DOG
TRAINING
BIBLE

All You Need to Know to Affordably and Playfully Raise the Best Companion Ever from Puppy to Adult Using the Power of Mental Exercise, Positive Reinforcement, and Healthy DIY Meal Plans

+4 BONUSES INCLUDED

- *HAPPY GOOD CITIZEN EXERCISE PROGRAM*
- *HOMEMADE DOG TOYS CRAFTING FOR INDOOR AND OUTDOOR PLAY GAMES*
- *SECRETS FOR PERFECT TRIPS WITH YOUR FAMILY COMPANION*
- *DOG TRAINING FOR KIDS*

CHARLOTTE MARLEY

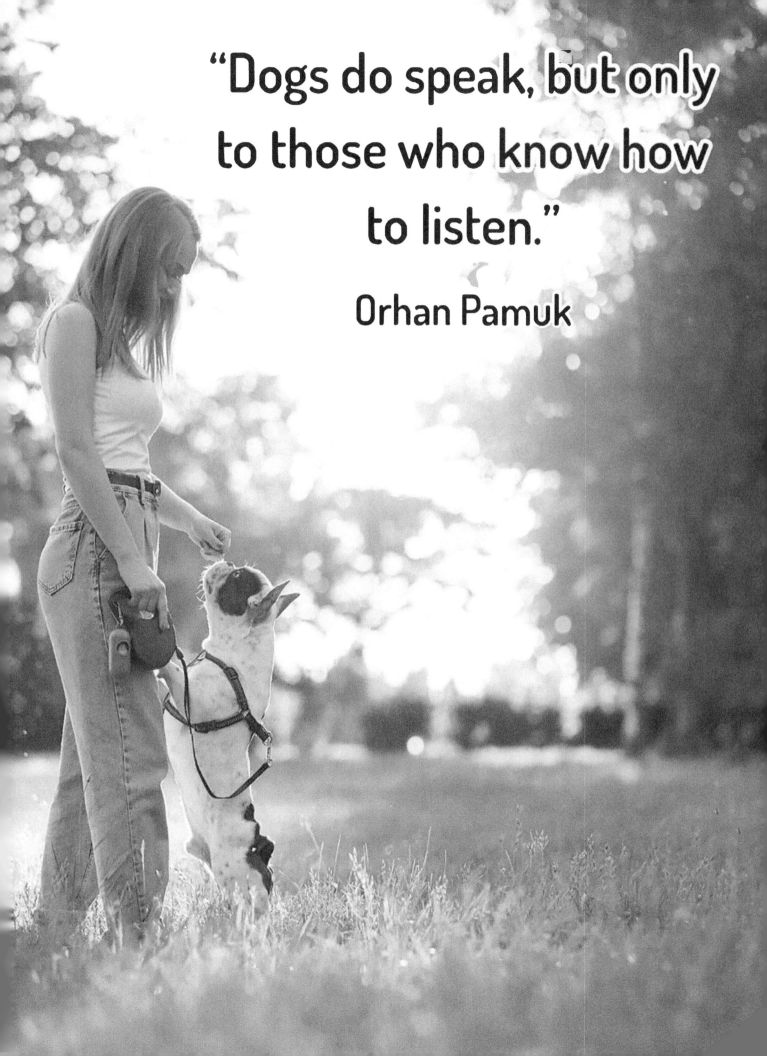

"Dogs do speak, but only to those who know how to listen."

Orhan Pamuk

TABLE OF CONTENTS

INTRODUCTION

Welcome to the "Dog Training Bible" – the ultimate guide to unlocking the full potential of the beautiful bond between you and your beloved canine companion. Charlotte Marley, an esteemed dog trainer, Starmark Academy-trained Behavior Specialist, and true "Canine Guru" has poured her heart and soul into this comprehensive guide. With over 20 years of experience in the field of dog training and behavior, she has developed the *"**Well-Behaved Companion Program**"*, which is a groundbreaking approach that combines positive reinforcement with psycho-attitudinal balance to transform the dog-owner relationship.

Throughout her illustrious career, Charlotte has helped countless dogs and their owners find happiness, harmony, and improved quality of life, both physically and psychologically. Her mission has always been to strengthen the understanding and connection between dogs and their humans, and the "Dog Training Bible" is her testament to that passion.

This book is designed for every dog owner, whether you're a first-time parent to a precious pup or an experienced handler looking to refine your skills. This book is divided into five comprehensive sections, guiding you step-by-step on your jour-ney towards a deeper bond with your furry friend.

1. **Home Preparation** – Create a safe, nurturing environment for your dog to thrive in, setting the stage for a healthy, happy life together.

2. **Buying Guide** – Learn how to choose the perfect breed for your lifestyle, and navigate the world of dog ownership responsibly.

3. **Puppy Training** – Discover essential techniques and gentle approaches to mold your puppy into a well-behaved, confident, and loving companion.

4. **Health and Wellbeing** – Prioritize your dog's physical and emotional health, ensuring a long, fulfilling life by your side.

5.   **Dog Tricks** – Master fun and engaging tricks that will not only entertain your friends and family but also strengthen the trust and communication between you and your dog.

This is more than just a book – it's a roadmap to a deeper understanding of your dog's mind and heart, a foundation for an unbreakable bond, and a testament to the profound love and respect that defines the relationship between humans and their canine companions. Dive into these pages and embark on an incredible jour-ney with Charlotte Marley as your guide, and witness the transformative power of her method as it brings joy, harmony, and unparalleled connection into your life with your four-legged friend.

It only remains for me to wish you a pleasant journey through the pages that fol-low, and to put it in the words of renowned veterinarian and author Nicholas H. Dod-man: *"Dogs are man's best friend, the least we can do is understand them a little better."*

Have a good read,

WBC Program Team

PART I

DOG-PROOFING YOUR HOME

"The better I get to know men, the more I find myself loving dogs."
– Charles De Gaulle

It's an exciting and rewarding experience to welcome a dog into your home. It also entails the responsibility of making your home a safe and comfortable environment for your new furry family member. This chapter will give you important guidelines and practical tips for dog-proofing your home's indoor and outdoor spaces, covering key areas such as living areas, kitchen and bathroom, bedrooms, fencing and boundaries, garden and yard, and pool and water safety. We'll also go over the importance of regular maintenance and monitoring, as well as how to adapt your dog-proofing measures as your dog grows and develops. By following the advice in this chapter, you will be well-equipped to provide a safe haven for your canine companion, promoting their well-being and strengthening your bond with your beloved pet.

The Importance of Dog-Proofing Your Home

When you welcome a dog into your home, you are not only adding a new member to your family but also taking on the responsibility of providing a secure and nurturing environment for your furry friend. Dog-proofing your home is a crucial aspect of responsible dog ownership, as it safeguards your canine companion from potential hazards and ensures their comfort and well-being. Without further ado, let's delve into the importance of dog-proofing and provides insights into creating a safe and comfortable environment for your dog to thrive.

One of the main reasons to dog-proof your home is to prevent accidents and injuries that may stem from your dog's natural curiosity and energetic nature. Dogs love to explore their surroundings, and while this curiosity is endearing, it can also lead them to encounter hazards within your home. By identifying and addressing potential dangers, you can significantly reduce the risk of your dog getting hurt or ingesting something harmful.

Moreover, creating a well-organized and secure environment can alleviate your dog's stress and anxiety. When your dog feels safe and comfortable in their surroundings, they are less likely to exhibit destructive behaviors or suffer from behavioral issues resulting from fear or anxiety. A calm, orderly living space contributes to their emotional stability and overall happiness. A secure and cozy environment stimulates your furry friend to have a healthy lifestyle. By facilitating a secure space, you encourage your dog to engage in healthy activities such as play, exploration, and rest. A well-planned living space nurtures their physical and mental well-being, fostering a balanced and contented lifestyle.

Lastly, dog-proofing your home not only protects your canine companion but also safeguards your belongings. By securing potentially hazardous items and designating safe zones for your dog, you minimize the likelihood of damage to your possessions while simultaneously ensuring your dog's safety.

Creating a Safe Haven for Your Canine Companion

To establish an optimal environment for your dog, it's essential to first understand your dog's unique needs and behaviors. Consider factors such as breed, age, size, and temperament when dog-proofing your home, as each dog is different and may require specific accommodations. For instance, larger dogs may need more space to move around, while smaller breeds might necessitate additional protection from potential hazards. Another critical component in creating a safe and comfortable space for your dog is setting clear boundaries. By designating specific areas for eating, sleeping, and playing, you help your dog develop a sense of routine and security. Providing a comfortable bed, a defined feeding area, and safe toys will make your dog feel at home and reduce the chances of them engaging in destructive behaviors.

As your dog matures and their needs evolve, it's vital to reassess your dog-proofing measures regularly. Continuously evaluate your home's safety features to ensure they remain suitable for your dog's changing requirements. For example, puppies often require extra precautions to protect them from potential hazards, while senior dogs might need adjustments to address mobility issues associated with aging.

Lastly, creating a safe environment for your dog extends beyond physical modifications. It also involves educating family members and visitors on interacting with your dog in a safe and respectful manner. Establish clear guidelines and boundaries for handling your dog, reinforcing positive behaviors, and discouraging inappropriate interactions. This strategy will support keeping your home's atmosphere peaceful and safe.

Indoor Dog-Proofing

As a pet owner, it is important to ensure that your furry friend has a secure and comfortable living space. Indoor dog-proofing is a crucial step in maintaining a safe environment for both your dog and your belongings. By taking the necessary precautions, you can prevent accidents and promote a peaceful relationship with your canine companion. In the following few lines I'll provide detailed guidance on how to make your living areas, kitchen, bathroom, and bedrooms safe and comfortable for your four-legged friend(s).

Living Areas

The living area is a central part of your home where you and your dog will spend a significant amount of time together. It is crucial to make sure that this area is secure and comfortable.

- Secure electrical cords and outlets: Dogs can be naturally curious, and loose electrical cords can pose a risk of electrocution or strangulation. To prevent accidents, hide cords behind furniture, use cable organizers, or encase them in protective covers. Additionally, consider using outlet covers to prevent your dog from coming into contact with live electrical sockets.

- Remove or secure potential choking hazards: Small objects such as coins, children's toys, and remote control batteries can pose choking hazards for your dog. Regularly inspect your living area and remove or secure any small items that your dog might be tempted to chew or swallow. Keeping your living space tidy and clutter-free is not only beneficial for your dog's safety but also helps maintain a pleasant environment for the whole family.

- Keep toxic plants out of reach: If consumed by dogs, several common houseplants can be poisonous. Research the plants in your home to determine if they are safe for your pet, and either remove toxic plants or place them in areas that are inaccessible to your dog. Ensure that your dog cannot reach hanging plants or climb onto surfaces where plants are displayed.

- Secure trashcans: Puppies are attracted to the smells coming from garbage, which can upset their health and be poisonous.

Kitchen and Bathroom

The kitchen and bathroom are particularly important areas to dog-proof, as they often contain potentially harmful substances and objects.

- Use child-proof locks on cabinets: Install child-proof locks on cabinets and drawers that store cleaning supplies, medications, and other hazardous items. This simple step can prevent your dog from accidentally accessing and ingesting dangerous substances.

- Store cleaning supplies and medications safely: Keep all cleaning supplies, medications, and other potentially toxic items in secure, high cabinets that are out of your dog's reach. When using these products, always follow the manufacturer's instructions and ensure that your dog is in a safe location away from the area being cleaned.

- Keep trash cans secure: Dogs are notorious for rummaging through trash cans in search of food scraps or intriguing scents. Invest in a sturdy, dog-proof trash can with a secure lid to prevent your dog from accessing its contents. This not only protects your dog from ingesting harmful items but also helps maintain a clean and hygienic living environment.

Bedrooms

Your bedroom is a place of rest and relaxation, and ensuring its safety for your dog is essential for their well-being.

- Provide a designated sleeping area: Set up a comfortable sleeping area for your dog, either within your bedroom or in a separate space. A cozy bed, blanket, or crate will give your dog a sense of security and comfort, and help establish a consistent bedtime routine.

- Keep personal items out of reach: Dogs may be tempted to chew on clothing, shoes, and other personal belongings. To prevent damage to your items and potential hazards for your dog, keep your personal belongings out of reach or stored away when not in use.

- Minimize loose fabrics and potential hazards: Inspect your bedroom for any loose fabrics or objects that could pose a risk to your dog, such as cords from blinds, curtains, or bedding. Secure or remove these items to ensure your dog's safety while in your bedroom. Check for any little items that can be choking dangers as well, and store them safely.

Indoor dog-proofing is an essential aspect of responsible dog ownership, contributing to the safety and well-being of your beloved canine companion. By following these guidelines and regularly reevaluating the safety measures in your home, you can create a nurturing environment where your dog can thrive, and both you and your pet can enjoy a happy and healthy life together. Now let's take a look at tips for dog-proofing outdoor environments!

Outdoor Dog-Proofing

Providing a secure and enjoyable outdoor environment for your furry friend is an essential responsibility of being a dog owner. Outdoor dog-proofing helps ensure that your pet can safely explore, play, and relax in a protected setting, while reducing the risk of accidents and injuries.

Fencing and Boundaries
A secure outdoor space starts with establishing clear and safe boundaries for your dog. Proper fencing and boundary systems prevent your dog from wandering off, keeping them secure within the confines of your property.

- Install secure and appropriate fencing: Choose fencing that is suitable for your dog's size, breed, and temperament. Make sure the fence is strong enough to hold your dog's weight and activity level and tall enough to prevent them from jumping over it. Materials such as wood, metal, or vinyl are popular choices for dog-proof fencing.

- Check for gaps and potential escape routes: Regularly inspect your fence for gaps, loose panels, or signs of wear and tear. To prevent your dog from falling through or being hurt, fix or replace any damaged pieces. Also, check for potential escape routes under the fence and fill in any gaps or install a barrier to prevent digging.

- Consider dog-specific boundary systems: In addition to physical fencing, you might consider installing dog-specific boundary systems, such as invisible or electric fences. These systems utilize a transmitter and a collar worn by your dog to establish an invisible boundary. Your dog will get a signal or a light correction if they go too close to the boundary. Always consult with a professional and follow the manufacturer's guidelines when installing and using these systems.

Garden and Yard

Your garden and yard should provide a safe and stimulating environment for your dog to explore and enjoy.

- Remove toxic plants and garden chemicals: Many common garden plants like Azalea, Begonia, Cyclamen or Tulip can be harmful to dogs if ingested. Research which plants are toxic and remove them from your garden or place them in areas inaccessible to your dog. Also, store garden chemicals, such as fertilizers and pesticides, in secure locations out of your dog's reach.

- Provide safe, designated digging areas: Dogs often enjoy digging, and providing a designated digging area can help channel this natural behavior while protecting your garden. Create a sandbox or a specific area filled with soft soil for your dog to dig in, and encourage them to use this area by burying treats or toys for them to discover.

- Secure outdoor furniture and decorations: Ensure that outdoor furniture, decorations, and other items are stable and secure to prevent accidents or injuries. Check for sharp edges, loose parts, or potential choking hazards, and remove or secure any items that could pose a risk to your dog.

Pool and Water Safety

If your property includes a pool or water feature, it's essential to take precautions to ensure your dog's safety around water.

- Install fencing or covers around pools and water features: Enclose pools and water features with secure fencing or use sturdy pool covers to prevent your dog from accidentally falling in. Consider installing self-closing gates and alarms to alert you if your dog enters the pool area unsupervised.

- Provide dog-specific life vests and flotation devices: When your dog is near water, consider using a dog-specific life vest or flotation device to help them stay afloat and reduce the risk of drowning. Choose a device that fits your dog comfortably and securely, and always supervise them while wearing the device.

- Teach your dog water safety and supervised swimming: Introduce your dog to water gradually and in a controlled environment. Teach them the fundamentals of swimming with confidence and properly entering and exiting the water. Always supervise your dog when they are near water, and consider enrolling them in a dog-specific swimming or water safety class to further enhance their skills and confidence.

If you are a responsible dog owner, it is important to prioritize outdoor dog-proofing to ensure a safe and enjoyable environment for your beloved pet. You can make your outside space a safe and nurturing environment for your furry buddy to thrive in by taking the required steps to dog-proof it. This will enhance their wellbeing and contribute to solidifying your relationship with your canine companion.

Regular Maintenance and Monitoring

Any pet owner's number one concern is the safety of their four-legged companion. This means that dog-proofing your home and outdoor environment should be an ongoing responsibility that requires regular maintenance and monitoring. Your dog's requirements, actions, and talents will vary as they mature and develop. Therefore, it's essential to adapt your dog-proofing measures accordingly. It's important to periodically inspect your home for new hazards, stay up-to-date with dog safety recommendations, and adjust your dog-proofing measures as your dog matures. You can keep your dog secure and content by adopting these precautions.

Periodically Inspect Your Home for New Hazards

Over time, your home and outdoor environment may accumulate new hazards that could pose a risk to your dog's safety. Regular inspections are crucial for identifying and addressing these hazards before they cause harm.

- Schedule routine inspections: Set a schedule for conducting thorough inspections of your home and outdoor spaces, such as monthly or seasonally. Consistent inspections will help ensure that your dog-proofing measures remain effective and your home remains safe for your pet.

- Assess each area systematically: During your inspections, examine each area of your home and outdoor environment, looking for potential hazards such as loose cords, damaged fencing, or new toxic plants. Address any issues immediately to prevent accidents or injuries.

- Involve the whole family: Encourage every family member to participate in maintaining a safe environment for your dog. Teach children how to rec-

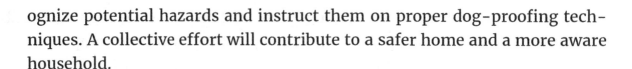

ognize potential hazards and instruct them on proper dog-proofing techniques. A collective effort will contribute to a safer home and a more aware household.

Keep Up-to-Date with Dog Safety Recommendations

As research and knowledge evolve, so do recommendations for dog safety. Staying informed about current best practices in dog-proofing will help ensure the continued well-being of your canine companion.

- Consult trusted sources: Regularly consult reliable sources of information, such as veterinary organizations, dog trainers, and pet safety experts, to stay informed about the latest dog safety recommendations. Books, websites, and social media channels can provide valuable insights and updates.

- Attend seminars or workshops: Participate in local seminars, workshops, or training classes focused on dog safety and dog-proofing. These events offer an opportunity to learn from professionals and connect with other dog owners who share your commitment to dog safety.

- Join online communities: Engage with online communities, forums, or social media groups dedicated to dog safety and care. You can ask questions, exchange experiences, and gain knowledge from other dog owners and professionals using these sites.

Adjust Dog-Proofing Measures as Your Dog Grows and Develops

Your dog's size, strength, and abilities will change as they grow and mature. It's crucial to adapt your dog-proofing measures to meet their evolving needs and ensure their continued safety.

- Monitor your dog's development: Regularly observe your dog's growth, behavior, and abilities. Pay attention to any changes that may necessitate adjustments in your dog-proofing measures, such as increased strength, agility, or curiosity.

- Update and modify dog-proofing measures: As your dog grows, you may need to modify your dog-proofing efforts. This could include raising the height of fences, securing larger or heavier items, or addressing new behavioral challenges, such as excessive chewing or digging.

- Consult with professionals: As your dog matures, it's a good idea to consult with your veterinarian, dog trainer, or a pet behavior specialist to discuss any concerns or questions regarding your dog's development and the effectiveness of your dog-proofing measures.

To keep your beloved dog safe, it is crucial to regularly assess and adjust your dog-proofing measures. This entails scrutinizing your living space for any potential dangers, staying up-to-date on the latest dog safety guidelines, and modifying your precautions as your dog grows and evolves. By making a little effort, you can ensure that your furry friend remains unharmed and protected.

In conclusion, dog-proofing is a crucial component of ethical pet ownership that fosters security, wellbeing, and a deep link between dogs and their owners. By maintaining a secure environment, staying informed about dog safety recommendations, and adapting your dog-proofing measures as your dog matures, you can create a nurturing space in which your furry companion can thrive. The result is a happy, healthy, and well-adjusted pet and a more fulfilling relationship between you and your beloved canine companion.

The next section of this comprehensive guide is called the "*Purchasing Guide*". Choosing the right dog to be a part of your family is just as important as creating a safe environment for them. Our upcoming section will provide detailed information on various factors to consider while planning to bring a furry friend into your life. We'll discuss everything from assessing your lifestyle and environment, understanding the breed characteristics, to financial implications, and even adopting versus purchasing from a breeder. We will also delve into the world of dog breeds, analyzing their temperament, trainability, grooming needs, and much more.

PART II
PURCHASING GUIDE

"A dog is the only thing on earth that loves you more than he loves himself."
—Josh Billings

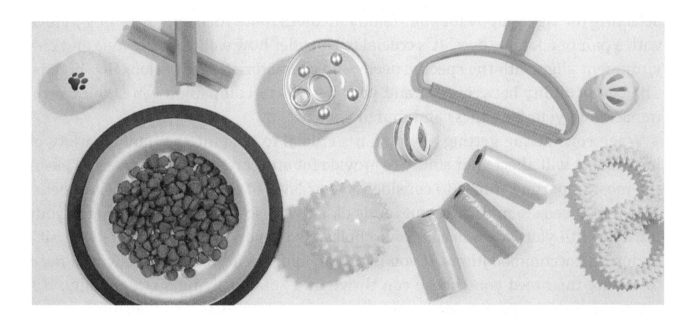

As you embark on the journey of welcoming a furry companion into your life, it's crucial to make well-informed decisions every step of the way. In this comprehensive purchasing guide, we cover essential topics, ranging from assessing your lifestyle and environment to understanding the financial implications of owning a dog. Additionally, you'll discover the importance of family dynamics and special considerations, ensuring a harmonious match between your new pet and your unique circumstances.

Moreover, we delve into the world of breed characteristics and provide a snapshot of the top 15 popular dog breeds, offering insights into their temperament, trainability, and care requirements. We examine the benefits and drawbacks of adopting from a shelter or rescue group versus buying from a reputable breeder to assist you in making an ethical decision. Lastly, we provide a checklist of essential equipment for your new puppy, ensuring you have everything you need to create a comfortable and loving home for your canine companion. With this guide, you'll be well-equipped to make informed decisions and pave the way for a fulfilling and long-lasting bond with your new best friend.

Assessing Your Lifestyle and Environment

Selecting the right puppy for your family involves more than simply falling in love with a pair of adorable eyes. It's crucial to consider how well your lifestyle and environment align with the specific needs and characteristics of various dog breeds. The compatibility between you and your new furry companion can significantly impact both your happiness and that of your pet.

When considering getting a puppy, it's crucial to take into account a variety of factors that will affect your ability to provide for and care for them properly. One of the most important things to consider is your level of activity and exercise needs. Different breeds require different levels of activity, so it's essential to match your lifestyle with your dog's needs. Your choice also depends a lot on your living situation and accommodations. If you live in an apartment, for example, you'll need to ensure the breed you choose can thrive in a smaller living space. Finally, it's crucial to consider your time commitment and availability when choosing a puppy. *Can you commit to training and spending time with a new puppy?* Otherwise, this might not be the ideal moment to bring one home. You can discover the ideal furry companion for your particular situation by taking these things into account.

Activity Level and Exercise Needs

When it comes to choosing the right puppy, one of the most important factors to consider is the amount of daily exercise and activity that both you and your potential dog can handle. Depending on their breed, age, and temperament, dogs have different exercise needs. Begin by evaluating your current activity level and how much time you can dedicate to exercising and playing with your dog. *Are you an outdoorsy, active person, or do you choose a more sedentary way of life?* Regarding your capacity and willingness to fulfill your dog's exercise requirements, be honest with yourself.

It's essential to research breed-specific exercise requirements, as different dog breeds have distinct needs. Some breeds, like Border Collies and Labrador Retrievers, require vigorous exercise and mental stimulation, while others, such as Greyhounds and Basset Hounds, are content with more moderate activity. Make sure that the breed you choose aligns with your activity level and the amount of exercise you can provide.

Keep in mind that puppies have different exercise needs than adult dogs. As your dog grows, their exercise requirements may change. Be prepared to modify your way of life to suit your dog's requirements at every stage of their existence.

Living Space and Accommodations

Your living space plays a significant role in determining the best breed or type of dog for your family. It's essential to choose a dog that can comfortably and safely live in your home environment. Start by assessing your available space, considering the size of your home, yard, and any outdoor areas where your dog will spend time. Some breeds, like Great Danes, require ample space to move around, while smaller breeds, such as Pugs or Chihuahuas, may be more suitable for apartment living.

Be aware of any housing restrictions or breed-specific legislation in your area. Some apartments, condos, or neighborhoods may have restrictions on dog size, breed, or the number of pets allowed. You can use this information to assist you decide which breed to choose. Lastly, ensure that your home has appropriate accommodations for your chosen breed. This may include secure fencing, a designated sleeping area, and sufficient room for exercise and play.

Time Commitment and Availability

Owning a dog requires a significant time commitment for daily care, training, and bonding. When selecting a puppy, it's crucial to evaluate your schedule and availability to ensure that you can meet the needs of your new pet. Reflect on your typical daily schedule and how a dog would fit into your life. *Can you find the time to provide your dog the food, exercise, grooming, and training that he or she needs?* Be realistic about the adjustments you may need to make to your routine to properly care for your new pet.

Assess your work schedule and any frequent travel commitments. If you have a demanding job or travel often, you may need to consider dog breeds that are more independent or can adapt to longer periods alone. Alternatively, you may need to arrange for pet sitters, dog walkers, or doggy daycare services to help care for your dog during your absence.

Family Dynamics and Special Considerations

When it comes to selecting the perfect puppy for your home, it's important to consider your family's specific circumstances. You'll want to take into account things like how well the puppy will get along with children and elderly family members, as well as any accommodations that may need to be made for family members with disabilities or allergies. By carefully evaluating these factors, you can ensure that the new addition to your family will fit right in and bring joy to everyone involved.

Compatibility with Children
The presence of children in your household is an important factor to consider when choosing the right puppy. While some breeds tend to be more quiet or timid, others are more naturally kind, patient, and tolerant of children. Look into breeds that are noted for having child-friendly temperaments to make sure your new pet and kids get along well. It's also important to teach your children how to interact safely and respectfully with dogs, as this will contribute to a positive relationship between them and your new puppy.

Interaction with Elderly Family Members
If you have elderly family members living in your household, it's essential to consider how your new puppy will interact with them. Some dog breeds are more adaptable and easygoing around older adults, while others may be too energetic or boisterous. When selecting a breed, look for those that are known for their calm

and gentle nature, and that can adapt to a slower-paced lifestyle. Additionally, consider the size and strength of the dog, as a large, rambunctious puppy may accidentally knock over or injure an older family member.

Accommodating Family Members with Disabilities

When choosing a puppy for a household with family members with disabilities, it's crucial to consider how the dog's temperament, size, and energy level will impact their ability to coexist safely and comfortably with those who have special needs. Some breeds are better suited for service or therapy roles, while others may be more challenging to manage for individuals with disabilities. Conduct thorough research to identify breeds that have the right combination of traits to ensure a successful relationship with your new pet.

Allergies and Hypoallergenic Breeds

For families with members who suffer from allergies, selecting a hypoallergenic breed can significantly improve their quality of life. Less allergens are produced by hypoallergenic breeds, which can lessen the likelihood that sensitive people will experience allergic reactions. The Maltese, Poodle, and Bichon Frise are a few breeds that are hypoallergenic. Keep in mind that no breed is completely allergen-free, but these breeds are less likely to trigger allergic reactions.

Financial Considerations

Before bringing a new furry friend into your home, it's important to understand the financial obligations associated with dog ownership. Owning a dog can require a significant financial commitment, so it's crucial to be aware of the various costs involved. In this chapter, we will cover the financial considerations associated with dog ownership, including the general expenses of owning a dog, healthcare and insurance costs, and breed-specific expenses such as grooming and training. You may make sure that you're totally ready for the responsibilities that come with dog ownership by developing a firm awareness of these financial factors.

Costs of Owning a Dog

When considering the financial implications of dog ownership, it's essential to account for both the initial costs and ongoing expenses. Initial costs include the purchase or adoption fee, vaccinations, microchipping, spaying or neutering, and basic supplies such as a crate, collar, leash, food and water dishes, and toys. Depending on your puppy's breed and where it came from, these upfront fees could be anything from a few hundred and several thousand dollars.

Ongoing expenses are another crucial aspect of dog ownership. These costs include food, grooming, routine veterinary care, flea and tick prevention, and annual vaccinations. You should also plan for unforeseen costs, such as urgent veterinarian care or repairing broken household items. The annual cost of dog ownership can range from $500 to over $2,000, depending on factors such as the size of the dog, the cost of living in your area, and the quality of food and supplies you choose.

Healthcare and Insurance Expenses

Healthcare expenses are a significant aspect of dog ownership, as maintaining your dog's health is essential for their overall well-being. Routine veterinary care, including annual checkups, vaccinations, and dental cleanings, can add up over time. Additionally, dogs may require more extensive medical care due to illness or injury, which can result in substantial costs.

Many pet owners opt to buy pet insurance in order to reduce these costs. Depending on the plan you choose, pet insurance may help pay for some of your dog's medical costs. When contemplating pet insurance, compare many providers and policies to choose the one that best meets your requirements and financial situation. Keep in mind that premiums, deductibles, and coverage levels vary between providers and plans, so it's essential to carefully evaluate your options.

If you need to compare the market to find the best pet insurance there are many usefull websites here you can find an example easy to use:

https://www.comparethemarket.com/pet-insurance/

Breed-Specific Expenses

Some dog breeds have unique expenses that should be considered when choosing a puppy. For example, certain breeds require regular grooming to maintain their coat and prevent matting, which can add to your monthly expenses. Breeds such as Poodles or Shih Tzus may need professional grooming every four to eight weeks, while breeds like Labrador Retrievers or Beagles have lower grooming needs.

Additionally, some breeds may require specialized training or more extensive socialization, which can also contribute to your overall expenses. For example, working breeds like Border Collies or German Shepherds may benefit from advanced training or dog sports to keep them mentally stimulated and well-behaved.

Adopting vs. Purchasing from a Breeder

When it comes to selecting the perfect puppy for your individual situation, it's essential to weigh the pros and cons of adopting from a shelter or rescue organization versus purchasing from a reputable breeder. Each option offers its own benefits, and taking the time to understand them can help you make the right choice for your family.

Adopting from a Shelter or Rescue Organization

Puppy adoption from a shelter or rescue group has various advantages. Firstly, you are providing a loving home to a dog in need, helping to alleviate the problem of pet overpopulation and overcrowding in shelters. These puppies are ready to find a forever home since they have frequently been abandoned or turned in as a result of events beyond their control.

Because adoption fees are typically lower than the price of a purebred puppy, adopting from a shelter or rescue group can also be more affordable than buying from a breeder. Additionally, many shelters and rescues provide initial veterinary care, including vaccinations and spaying or neutering, as part of the adoption process. Finally, adopting from a shelter or rescue organization can provide you with a wider range of options in terms of breed, age, and temperament. This diversity allows you to select a puppy that best fits your unique circumstances and preferences.

Selecting Reputable Breeders

Finding a reputable breeder who puts their dogs' health and welfare first is essential if you decide to buy a puppy from a breeder. A trustworthy breeder will thoroughly check their breeding stock for genetic health problems, give their puppies a clean and loving environment, and take measures to socialize and get the puppies ready for their new homes.

Ask for references from previous clients when researching breeders, and look for referrals from reputable organizations like veterinary clinics or breed clubs. Visit the breeder's location to see the surroundings in which the puppies are raised and to inquire about the pedigree, medical history, and any warranties they may be offering.

Consider the ethical ramifications of your choice before deciding whether to adopt a puppy or purchase one from a breeder. By giving a needy puppy a second chance, you can fight pet overpopulation by adopting from a shelter or rescue group. On the other hand, buying from a reputable breeder can help promote ethical breeding methods and support the preservation of particular breed characteristics. It's imperative to avoid supporting unethical activities like puppy mills or backyard breeders who put profit before animal welfare, regardless of the course you take. By making a thoughtful and well-informed choice, you can support moral dog ownership and protect the breed's future.

Evaluating Breed Characteristics

It is crucial to consider the breed's characteristics when searching for the perfect puppy for your family. These factors will have a significant impact on your future life together. This section covers various breed traits, including size and growth potential, temperament and personality traits, trainability and intelligence, and grooming and maintenance requirements. By examining these factors and providing realistic examples and practical references, you can make an informed decision when selecting the ideal puppy for your unique circumstances.

Size and Growth Potential

The size and growth potential of a dog breed can have a significant impact on your home environment, the dog's exercise needs, and the overall cost of ownership. For example, a small breed like the Chihuahua will require less living space, making them more suitable for apartment living. In contrast, a larger breed like the Great Dane will need more room to move around comfortably and might not be the best fit for smaller living spaces.

Consider your living environment and whether the size of a specific breed will be appropriate with your lifestyle when considering size and development potential. For example, if you have little children, a medium-sized breed, such as a Golden Retriever, may be more ideal than a small or large breed due to their solid structure and gentle demeanor.

Temperament and Personality Traits

A dog's temperament and personality traits play a crucial role in determining the compatibility between the dog and your family. Some breeds, such as the Labrador Retriever, are well renowned for their outgoing and sociable personalities, which makes them excellent family dogs. Other breeds, like the Shiba Inu, have a more reserved and independent personality, which might not be the best fit for a household with young children.

Think about the personalities that would best fit your family and your way of life when assessing a breed's temperament. A high-energy breed like the Border Collie, for instance, can be a fantastic fit if you're an outdoorsy, active person. A laid-back breed like the Bulldog, on the other hand, would be a better fit if you like a more easygoing way of life.

Trainability and Intelligence

A dog's trainability and intelligence can significantly impact your experience as a dog owner. Some breeds, like the Poodle or the German Shepherd, are known for their exceptional intelligence and trainability, making them suitable for various activities, including obedience training, agility, and search and rescue work.

When considering a breed's trainability and intelligence, think about your training goals and the amount of time you're willing to invest in your dog's education. For example, if you're interested in participating in dog sports or advanced obedience training, a breed with high trainability and intelligence might be the best choice. Conversely, if you're looking for a companion with minimal training needs, a breed like the Beagle or the Dachshund may be more suitable.

Grooming and Maintenance Requirements

Finally, a breed's grooming and maintenance requirements can impact the time and effort you'll need to invest in your dog's care. Breeds like the Poodle or the Afghan Hound require regular grooming to maintain their coats and prevent matting, while short-haired breeds like the Boxer or the Greyhound have minimal grooming needs.

Consider your willingness to devote time and money to your dog's care when assessing the grooming and maintenance requirements. Choose a breed that requires little grooming if you want a low-maintenance pet. However, if you're prepared to spend money on routine professional grooming, a breed with more demanding grooming needs might be right for you.

Top 15 Popular Dog Breeds: Characteristics & Care Essentials

When it comes to choosing a dog, it's important to consider a variety of factors in order to find the perfect fit for your lifestyle. One of the key considerations is the breed, as different breeds have different characteristics and traits that may make them better suited to certain homes and families. To help you in your search, we've compiled a list of 15 of the most common dog breeds, broken down by size and growth potential, temperament and personality traits, trainability and intelligence, and grooming and maintenance requirements. Keep in mind that while these are general guidelines, individual dogs within a breed may vary, so it's important to spend time with a puppy or adult dog before making a decision to ensure it's a good fit for your family and lifestyle.

Labrador Retriever

- *Size and growth potential:* Medium to large, 55–80 pounds
- *Temperament and personality traits:* Friendly, outgoing, and eager to please
- *Trainability and intelligence:* High
- *Grooming and maintenance requirements:* Moderate, regular brushing

German Shepherd

- *Size and growth potential:* Large, 50–90 pounds
- *Temperament and personality traits:* Loyal, intelligent, and protective
- *Trainability and intelligence:* High
- *Grooming and maintenance requirements:* Moderate to high, regular brushing and occasional grooming

Golden Retriever

- *Size and growth potential:* Medium to large, 55–75 pounds
- *Temperament and personality traits:* Friendly, intelligent, and affectionate
- *Trainability and intelligence:* High
- *Grooming and maintenance requirements:* Moderate to high, regular brushing and occasional grooming

French Bulldog

- *Size and growth potential:* Small to medium, 16–28 pounds
- *Temperament and personality traits:* Affectionate, easygoing, and adaptable
- *Trainability and intelligence:* Moderate
- *Grooming and maintenance requirements:* Low, minimal brushing

Bulldog

- *Size and growth potential:* Medium, 40–50 pounds
- *Temperament and personality traits:* Gentle, affectionate, and calm

- *Trainability and intelligence:* Moderate
- *Grooming and maintenance requirements:* Low to moderate, occasional brushing

Poodle (Standard, Miniature, and Toy)
- *Size and growth potential:* Varies, Toy (4-6 pounds), Miniature (10-15 pounds), Standard (40-70 pounds)
- *Temperament and personality traits:* Intelligent, friendly, and energetic
- *Trainability and intelligence:* High
- *Grooming and maintenance requirements:* High, regular professional grooming

Beagle
- *Size and growth potential:* Small to medium, 20-30 pounds
- *Temperament and personality traits:* Friendly, curious, and happy
- *Trainability and intelligence:* Moderate
- *Grooming and maintenance requirements:* Low, minimal brushing

Yorkshire Terrier
- *Size and growth potential:* Small, 4-7 pounds
- *Temperament and personality traits:* Affectionate, bold, and confident
- *Trainability and intelligence:* Moderate
- *Grooming and maintenance requirements:* Moderate to high, regular brushing and grooming

Boxer
- *Size and growth potential:* Medium to large, 55-70 pounds
- *Temperament and personality traits:* Playful, loyal, and protective
- *Trainability and intelligence:* Moderate
- *Grooming and maintenance requirements:* Low, minimal brushing

Dachshund

- *Size and growth potential:* Small, 16–32 pounds
- *Temperament and personality traits:* Lively, affectionate, and courageous
- *Trainability and intelligence:* Moderate
- *Grooming and maintenance requirements:* Varies, short-haired (low), long-haired (moderate), and wire-haired (moderate to high)

Siberian Husky

- *Size and growth potential:* Medium to large, 35–60 pounds
- *Temperament and personality traits:* Friendly, intelligent, and energetic
- *Trainability and intelligence:* Moderate
- *Grooming and maintenance requirements:* High, regular brushing and grooming

Rottweiler

- *Size and growth potential:* Large, 80–135 pounds
- *Temperament and personality traits:* Confident, loyal, and protective
- *Trainability and intelligence:* High
- *Grooming and maintenance requirements:* Low to moderate, occasional brushing

Shih Tzu

- *Size and growth potential:* Small, 9–16 pounds
- *Temperament and personality traits:* Affectionate, outgoing, and friendly
- *Trainability and intelligence:* Moderate
- *Grooming and maintenance requirements:* High, regular brushing and professional grooming

Border Collie

- *Size and growth potential:* Medium, 30–45 pounds
- *Temperament and personality traits:* Energetic, intelligent, and eager to please
- *Trainability and intelligence:* High

- *Grooming and maintenance requirements:* Moderate, regular brushing and occasional grooming

Chihuahua

- *Size and growth potential:* Small, 2-6 pounds
- *Temperament and personality traits:* Alert, spirited, and devoted
- *Trainability and intelligence:* Moderate
- *Grooming and maintenance requirements:* Varies, short-haired (low), long-haired (moderate)

Having trouble making a choice on the ideal dog breed for you? Take a look at the comparison of various dog breeds below to assess how their distinct characteristics and traits measure up against each other:

https://www.akc.org/compare-breeds/

Essential Equipment for Your New Puppy

It can be thrilling to be ready for a new puppy's arrival, but you must make sure you have all you need to keep your furry friend happy, secure, and healthy. There are a variety of items you'll need to gather before your puppy arrives, including food and water bowls, a collar and leash, a bed or crate, and toys to keep them entertained. It's important to choose high-quality products that are suited to your specific needs and lifestyle, so be sure to do your research and ask for recommendations from other pet owners or professionals. You can set yourself up to provide your new puppy a happy, healthy home with the correct supplies and a little bit of forethought.

Your puppy will need a cozy, secure place to sleep first and foremost. A top-notch dog bed is an investment in your dog's wellbeing because it gives them a special place to unwind and sleep. When selecting a bed, consider the size of your dog and the durability of the materials. Ideally, the bed should be large enough to accommodate your dog's growth but not too big that it overwhelms them. Choose beds with removable and washable coverings that are made of materials that are simple to clean. Blankets can be added for extra comfort, especially during colder months.

Feeding and drinking bowls are another essential item. Choose ceramic or stainless steel bowls over others since they are long-lasting, hygienic, and less prone to contain bacteria. Be sure to place the bowls in a location where your puppy can easily access them and where spills can be easily cleaned up. For puppies that tend to eat too quickly, slow-feed bowls are a great option to encourage a healthier pace during mealtimes.

When it comes to walking your puppy, a leash and harness or collar are crucial. For puppies, harnesses are typically advised because they evenly distribute pressure across the chest, lowering the chance of harm. When selecting a harness or collar, ensure it fits snugly but allows for two fingers to fit comfortably between the collar or harness and your dog's skin. As your puppy grows, you may need to adjust the size or purchase a new one to accommodate their growth. Don't forget to attach an identification tag with your contact information to the collar or harness.

It's a smart idea to have your puppy microchipped since it greatly enhances the likelihood that you'll find them again if they get lost. Most veterinarians and animal shelters can perform this simple procedure, which involves implanting a tiny microchip beneath your dog's skin. A unique identifying number that can be registered with a national database and used to connect your contact information to your dog is contained in the chip.

A crate or cage can be a valuable tool for house training and providing a safe, secure space for your puppy when you're unable to supervise them. Make sure the crate is big enough for your dog to comfortably lie down, stand up, and turn around, but not so big that it invites accidents. Making the crate a welcoming and comfortable setting for your puppy can help you introduce it gradually.

Toys are essential for your puppy's mental and physical stimulation. Provide a variety of toys, such as chew toys, plush toys, and puzzle toys, to keep your dog engaged and entertained. Rotate the toys regularly to maintain your puppy's interest. Make sure the toys you choose are made of sturdy, non-toxic materials and are the right size for the breed and age of your puppy. Training accessories, such as clickers, treat pouches, and target sticks, can help support your puppy's training and development. Choose tools that align with your preferred training method and use them consistently to reinforce desired behaviors.

Puppy Essentials Checklist

- ✓ **Dog bed**
  Sized appropriately for growth
  Easy-to-clean materials
- ✓ **Blankets (optional)**
  For added comfort and warmth
- ✓ **Feeding and drinking bowls**
  Stainless steel or ceramic
  Slow-feed bowls (if needed)
- ✓ **Leash and harness or collar**
  Properly fitted
  Identification tag with contact information
- ✓ **Microchipping**
  Performed by a veterinarian or animal shelter
  Register with a national database
- ✓ **Crate or cage**
  Large enough for comfort but not too big
  Gradually introduce as a positive environment
- ✓ **Toys**
  Variety (chew toys, plush toys, puzzle toys)
  Durable, non-toxic materials
  Appropriate size for breed and age
- ✓ **Training accessories (see below).**

Essential checklist to train your Puppy

An essential checklist for training your puppy includes several items.

- First, you'll need a sturdy leash made of materials like nylon, leather, or heavy cotton. It's important to create a positive association between your dog and the leash, which can make going for walks or car rides easier. Reward your dog with training treats when you clip the leash to their harness. Treats can also be helpful in redirecting their attention if they tend to chew

on the leash. Even if you have a secure property, leash training is necessary for vet visits and public spaces.

- Next, consider a flat-buckle or breakaway collar for your dog. Collars are useful for carrying identification and other necessary documents, but it's generally better to attach the leash to a harness rather than the collar. Collars should be loose enough to fit two fingers between the collar and your dog's skin to avoid strain or chafing. A collar alone is not sufficient for controlling or restraining your dog during walks.

- A properly-fitted front-clip harness is recommended for general activities such as walks and car rides. However, it should be taken off during play-time with other dogs or while in the house to prevent accidents. Improperly fitted harnesses or excessive wear can cause discomfort or even gait issues. Despite the debate, harnesses are still a safer option than leashes for re-straining dogs, as they eliminate the risk of neck damage.

- Using a training clicker is a personal choice, but it can aid in teaching your dog various behaviors. Clickers are inexpensive and can be found at pet supply stores or online. Alternatively, you can use any household object that produces a distinct clicking noise. The key is to develop a positive association with the sound for effective training.

- Delicious dog treats are essential for motivating and rewarding your dog during training exercises. Choose low-calorie, high-reward treats that your dog finds enticing. A successful training program requires a generous amount of treats, so it's important to find affordable, portable options that won't contribute to weight gain. Boiled chicken is a recommended training treat, but you can also consider using vegetables if your dog enjoys them.

Finally, it's crucial to avoid using certain training tools that can cause harm to your dog. These include choke collars, prong collars, head halters, and electric shock systems. Opt for positive reinforcement methods instead. I've found that regularly assessing and updating your puppy's equipment is crucial to ensuring their needs are being met as they grow. As puppies grow quickly, it's important to make sure their equipment, such as their collar and leash, fit properly and are appropriate for their size and activity level. Additionally, as their needs change, such as if they become more active or require different types of toys, it's important to update their equipment accordingly. By doing so, you can help keep your puppy safe, healthy, and happy.

The next sections cover various topics related to obedience training, including teaching your dog basic commands such as sit, stay, come, and heel. It also discusses how to address common behavior problems like jumping, barking, and digging. Additionally, this section provides tips on how to socialize your dog with other dogs and people and how to train them for specific activities like agility or therapy work.

PART III

PUPPY TRAINING

"Once you have had a wonderful dog, a life without one, is a life diminished."
—Dean Koontz

Understanding Your Puppy's Growth Stages

Young puppies present both exciting and difficult experiences for both new dog owners and their canine companions. Similar to kids, puppies go through different growth and development stages, each with its own distinct set of benchmarks and expectations. Understanding your puppy's developmental phases will help you better meet their physical, mental, and emotional demands.

Key Developmental Milestones

It's essential to be aware of the key developmental milestones in your puppy's life, as these will help you know when to introduce specific training and socialization activities.

- **Neonatal period (0-2 weeks):** During this stage, puppies are completely dependent on their mother for warmth, nourishment, and stimulation. Their eyes and ears are closed, and they primarily use their sense of touch and smell to navigate the world.

- **Transitional period (2-4 weeks):** Puppies start to investigate their surroundings, open their eyes and ears, and interact with their littermates at this period. They also start to develop motor skills, allowing them to move around more confidently.

- **Socialization period (4-14 weeks):** This crucial stage is when puppies are most receptive to new experiences, making it the perfect time to introduce them to a variety of people, animals, and environments. During this period, puppies will learn how to communicate with other dogs and humans, and they will start to understand basic commands.

- **Juvenile period (14 weeks-6 months):** As puppies enter the juvenile stage, they become more independent and curious. They will continue to learn and refine their social skills and should be enrolled in a puppy training class to reinforce good behaviors and curb any unwanted ones.

- **Adolescence (6-18 months):** During adolescence, puppies experience hormonal changes that may lead to increased energy levels, testing boundaries, and occasional stubbornness. It's essential to maintain consistent training and provide appropriate outlets for physical and mental stimulation during this stage.

What to Expect at Various Ages

Understanding what to expect at each stage of your puppy's growth can help you tailor your training approach and provide the support they need to thrive.

- **8-12 weeks:** At this age, puppies should be introduced to their new home and family. Begin teaching basic commands such as "sit," "stay," and "come" using positive reinforcement techniques. Start house training and crate training as well.

- **12-16 weeks:** Continue to reinforce basic commands and gradually introduce new ones. Socialization should be a priority during this time, exposing your puppy to a wide range of sights, sounds, and experiences. Begin leash training and encourage proper chewing habits with appropriate toys.

- **4-6 months:** As your puppy's energy levels increase, ensure they receive adequate exercise and playtime. Introduce more advanced commands and work on improving their recall skills. Be patient and consistent with house training, as accidents may still occur.

- **6-12 months:** This period may bring about some adolescent behaviors such as pushing boundaries and testing your patience. Maintain consistent training, positive reinforcement, and a structured routine to help your puppy navigate this stage.

You will be better prepared to give your puppy the essential training, socialization, and support they require to grow into a well-rounded, self-assured adult dog if you are aware of their growth stages and developmental milestones. Having a successful and joyful puppyhood requires patience, persistence, and a positive outlook.

Age-Appropriate Training for Your Puppy

It is absolutely imperative that you train your puppy in order to ensure that you have a well-behaved and well-adjusted furry friend. However, it is crucial to keep

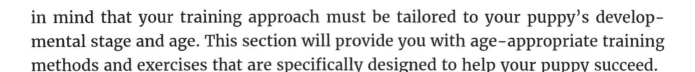

in mind that your training approach must be tailored to your puppy's developmental stage and age. This section will provide you with age-appropriate training methods and exercises that are specifically designed to help your puppy succeed.

8-12 weeks

During this stage, your puppy is eager to learn and highly receptive to new experiences. It's the ideal time to introduce them to basic obedience commands and start building a strong foundation for future training.

Crate training: Introduce your puppy to their crate by making it a comfortable and inviting space. Gradually increase the time they spend in the crate to help them feel secure and develop a positive association with it.

House training: Start house training by establishing a routine and taking your puppy out to the designated potty spot at regular intervals. Be patient and consistent, and remember to praise them when they go to the bathroom outside.

Basic commands: Begin teaching your puppy essential commands such as "sit," "stay," and "come." Use positive reinforcement, treats, and praise to reward your puppy for their efforts.

12-16 weeks

As your puppy grows, continue to reinforce the basic commands they've learned and introduce new ones.

Leash training: Familiarize your puppy with wearing a collar and leash by gradually introducing them to the sensation. Begin walking your puppy on a leash in a low-distraction environment, praising them for walking calmly by your side.

Socialization: Continue to expose your puppy to various sights, sounds, and experiences. Arrange playdates with other puppies and introduce them to different types of people, animals, and environments.

Chewing habits: Provide appropriate chew toys to encourage proper chewing habits and redirect any inappropriate chewing to suitable toys.

4-6 months

At this stage, your puppy's energy levels and curiosity will increase, making it essential to provide both physical and mental stimulation.

Advanced commands: Introduce more complex commands such as "heel," "leave it," and "off." Practice these commands in various environments to help your puppy generalize the behaviors.

Recall training: Work on improving your puppy's recall skills by practicing the "come" command in a safe, enclosed area with increasing levels of distraction.

Exercise and play: Ensure your puppy receives adequate daily exercise and playtime to help them burn off excess energy and prevent boredom-related behaviors.

6-12 months

During adolescence, your puppy may experience hormonal changes that can lead to boundary testing and occasional stubbornness.

Consistency and structure: Maintain a consistent training routine and structured schedule to help your puppy navigate this challenging stage.

Ongoing socialization: Continue to expose your puppy to new experiences and reinforce appropriate behaviors in various situations.

Enroll in a training class: Consider enrolling your puppy in an obedience or agility class to further refine their skills and provide an additional source of mental stimulation.

Positive Training Methods for Puppy Training

In the world of puppy training, positive training methods have become increasingly popular due to their effectiveness and humane approach. These methods focus on reinforcing desirable behaviors while minimizing the use of punishment or force. In this chapter, we will discuss the key components of positive training methods and how to apply them to your puppy's training sessions.

Positive Reinforcement

Positive reinforcement is the process of rewarding your puppy with something they like (such as treats, praise, or toys) immediately after they perform a desirable behavior. This reinforcement helps your puppy understand that their actions have positive consequences, making them more likely to repeat the behavior in the future. For example, when teaching your puppy to sit, you would reward them with a treat and praise as soon as their bottom touches the ground. Over time, your puppy will associate sitting with receiving rewards and will be more inclined to sit when asked.

Timing and Repetition

Timing and repetition are crucial aspects of successful puppy training. When using positive reinforcement, it's important to reward your puppy immediately after they perform the desired behavior. This helps your puppy make a clear connection between their action and the reward. Repetition is also essential in reinforcing your puppy's understanding of commands and behaviors. Consistently practicing and reinforcing desired behaviors will help solidify the training and ensure long-term success.

Appropriate Rewards (Treats)

Choosing the right rewards for your puppy is an important factor in positive training methods. High-value treats, such as small pieces of cooked chicken, cheese, or commercial dog treats, are often effective in capturing your puppy's attention and motivating them to perform. It's important to use small, easily consumable treats during training sessions to prevent your puppy from becoming too full or losing interest. Additionally, you can vary the types of treats you use to keep your puppy engaged and motivated.

Choosing the right rewards for your puppy is an important factor in positive training methods. High-value treats, such as small pieces of cooked chicken, cheese, or commercial dog treats, are often effective in capturing your puppy's attention and motivating them to perform. It's important to use small, easily consumable treats during training sessions to prevent your puppy from becoming too full or losing interest. Additionally, you can vary the types of treats you use to keep your puppy engaged and motivated.

Here are two homemade treats that have been proven to be highly attractive to dogs during training:

Liver Training Treats:

INGREDIENTS:
   1 pound of liver (chicken or beef)
   Water (for boiling)

INSTRUCTIONS:
-   Preheat your oven to 200°F (95°C) and line a baking sheet with parchment paper.
-   Rinse the liver under cold water to remove any excess blood or debris.
-   In a pot, bring water to a boil and add the liver. Boil for about 10 minutes until cooked through.
-   Remove the liver from the pot and allow it to cool slightly.
-   Cut the liver into small, bite-sized pieces.
-   Place the liver pieces on the prepared baking sheet and bake in the preheated oven for about 2-3 hours or until they become dry and chewy.
-   Once baked, let the liver treats cool completely before using them for training. Store in an airtight container in the refrigerator.
-   These liver treats are highly aromatic and irresistible to most dogs, making them an excellent choice for training rewards.

Cheese and Bacon Training Balls:

INGREDIENTS:
   1 cup grated cheddar cheese
   1/2 cup cooked bacon, crumbled

1/2 cup oat flour (or substitute with regular flour if preferred)

1 large egg

INSTRUCTIONS:

- Preheat your oven to 350°F (175°C) and line a baking sheet with parchment paper.
- In a mixing bowl, combine the grated cheddar cheese, crumbled bacon, oat flour, and egg. Mix well until a dough-like consistency forms.
- Take small portions of the mixture and roll them into bite-sized balls.
- Place the cheese and bacon balls on the prepared baking sheet and flatten them slightly with the back of a spoon.
- Bake in the preheated oven for approximately 15-20 minutes or until the treats are golden brown and firm.
- Allow the treats to cool completely before using them for training. Store in an airtight container in the refrigerator.
- These cheese and bacon training balls are rich in flavor and texture, making them highly enticing for dogs during training sessions.

Remember to consider any dietary restrictions or allergies your dog may have and adjust the ingredients accordingly.

Science-Based, Force-Free Training Techniques

Science-based, force-free training techniques prioritize understanding your puppy's natural behaviors and learning processes. These methods focus on teaching your puppy through positive reinforcement, rather than relying on punishment or force. By using force-free techniques, you can build a strong, trusting bond with your puppy and ensure their emotional well-being throughout the training process. Examples of science-based, force-free training techniques include clicker training, lure-reward training, and shaping. These methods encourage your puppy to think and learn, while also reinforcing their natural inclination to please you.

Effective Communication

A crucial aspect of positive training methods is learning to communicate effectively with your puppy. This involves understanding your puppy's body language and signals, as well as using clear, consistent verbal and non-verbal cues when training. To communicate effectively, it's important to use consistent commands and gestures for each behavior you're teaching. Additionally, being patient and observant will help you understand your puppy's signals and respond accordingly.

Crate Training

Crate training is an essential component of puppy training that offers numerous benefits to both you and your beloved companion. Crate training offers various advantages for both puppies and their owners, including:

- **Safety:** A crate provides a safe and secure space for your puppy, minimizing the risk of accidents or injuries when you are unable to supervise them.

- **House training:** Crates can help expedite the house-training process by taking advantage of a puppy's natural inclination to keep their sleeping area clean.

- **Travel:** A crate-trained puppy will be more comfortable and secure when traveling, whether it's a short trip to the vet or a longer journey.

- **Reduced anxiety:** A crate can serve as a comforting "den" for your puppy, reducing stress and anxiety in unfamiliar situations.

Introducing your puppy to their crate should be a gradual, positive experience. Follow these steps to ensure a smooth introduction:

1. **Choose the right crate** - Select a crate that is large enough for your puppy to stand up, turn around, and lie down comfortably. Look for a crate with adjustable dividers, allowing you to expand the space as your puppy grows.

2. **Make the crate inviting** - Create a cozy environment by placing a soft bed, blankets, and a few toys inside the crate. Ensure the crate is in a quiet, low-traffic area of your home, where your puppy can feel relaxed.

3. **Introduce your puppy to the crate** – Encourage your puppy to explore the crate by placing treats and toys inside. Leave the door open initially, allowing them to come and go as they please. Praise and reward your puppy when they voluntarily enter the crate.

4. **Gradual increments of time** – Once your puppy is comfortable entering the crate, begin closing the door for short periods. Start with just a few minutes and gradually increase the duration. Remember to reward your puppy with praise and treats for remaining calm inside the crate.

5. **Introduce meals in the crate** – Begin feeding your puppy their meals inside the crate. This will create a positive association with the crate and help them feel more at ease when the door is closed.

6. **Crate your puppy when you're home** – To prevent your puppy from associating the crate with your absence, practice crating them for short periods while you're home. This will help them understand that the crate is a safe space, even when you're nearby.

7. **Overnight crating** – Once your puppy is comfortable spending extended periods in their crate, begin crating them overnight. Place the crate in your bedroom or close by, so your puppy can sense your presence.

Potty Training

As a responsible pet owner, it's important to teach your furry friend the essential skill of potty training. Not only does it help keep your home clean and healthy, but it also ensures that your puppy can maintain good hygiene habits. This section offers a comprehensive guide on how to set a schedule, gradually introduce your puppy to potty training, and reinforce positive behavior using realistic examples and practical references. With patience and consistency, you can teach your puppy this important skill and enjoy a happy, healthy life together.

Setting a Schedule

Establishing a consistent schedule is vital for successful potty training. Puppies have small bladders, which means they need to eliminate frequently. Here's a basic outline to help you set up a potty schedule for your puppy:

- **First thing in the morning:** Take your puppy outside immediately after they wake up.

- **After meals:** Puppies usually need to eliminate 15-30 minutes after eating.

- **After naps:** Take your puppy out as soon as they wake up from a nap.

- **After playtime:** Excitement and physical activity can stimulate the need to eliminate.

- **Before bedtime:** Ensure your puppy goes potty before going to sleep for the night.

Keep in mind that young puppies may need to go outside every 1-2 hours during the day. As they grow older, their bladder control improves, and the frequency of potty breaks can be gradually reduced.

Potty training should be a gradual process, focusing on patience and positive reinforcement. Follow these steps for a smooth introduction:

Choose a desgnated potty area: Select a specific area outdoors where you want your puppy to eliminate. Consistently bringing them to the same spot will help them understand what is expected of them.

Use a cue word or phrase: Choose a cue word or phrase like "go potty" or "do your business" to signal your puppy that it's time to eliminate. Say the cue word when you take your puppy to the designated area.

Praise and reward: When your puppy successfully eliminates in the designated area, immediately praise and reward them with a treat. This promotes a favorable link between the desired behavior and the action.

Supervise and prevent accidents: Keep a close eye on your puppy when indoors. Take them outside right away if you see any indications that they need to go, like as sniffing, circling, or whining.

Manage accidents: Accidents are bound to happen during potty training. If you catch your puppy in the act, interrupt them with a firm "no" and take them outside to finish. Clean up the accident thoroughly to remove any lingering odors that might encourage future accidents.

Leash Training

Leash training is an essential skill for every dog, as it ensures their safety and comfort during walks and other outdoor activities. Before you can begin leash training, your puppy must become comfortable with wearing a collar or harness. Follow these steps to make the introduction smooth and positive:

- **Choose the right equipment:** Select a collar or harness that fits your puppy comfortably and securely. Adjustable options are ideal, as they can grow with your puppy. For the leash, choose a lightweight, non-retractable version to maintain control during training.

- **Gradual introduction:** Allow your puppy to sniff and investigate the collar or harness before putting it on. Once they seem comfortable, gently place the collar or harness on your puppy and reward them with praise or a treat. Allow your puppy to wear the collar or harness for short periods indoors, gradually increasing the duration.

- **Adding the leash:** Once your puppy is comfortable with the collar or harness, attach the leash and let them explore their surroundings while dragging the leash behind them (under supervision). This step helps your puppy become familiar with the sensation of the leash without the pressure of walking on it.

Teaching Loose-Leash Walking

Loose-leash walking means that your puppy walks calmly by your side without pulling on the leash or lagging behind. Teaching this skill requires patience and consistency. Here are the steps to get started:

1. **Start indoors:** Begin leash training indoors or in a familiar, low-distraction environment. Hold the leash in one hand and treats or a clicker in the other.

2. **Choose a cue:** Select a cue, such as "heel" or "let's go," that signals to your puppy that it's time to walk. Consistently use this cue throughout the training process.

3. **Reward proper positioning:** Encourage your puppy to walk by your side by rewarding them with treats or praise when they maintain the correct position. Stop moving and wait for them to come back to your side if they start to go forward. Avoid yanking or jerking the leash, as this can cause discomfort and fear.

4. **Practice turns and changes in direction:** Incorporate turns and changes in direction into your training sessions. This helps your puppy learn to pay attention to you and follow your lead. Reward them for maintaining proper positioning throughout these maneuvers.

5. **Gradually increase distractions:** As your puppy becomes more proficient with loose-leash walking, gradually introduce distractions, such as other dogs, people, or noises. Begin at a distance and work your way closer to the distractions, rewarding your puppy for maintaining focus and proper positioning.

6. **Be patient and consistent:** Loose-leash walking takes time and practice to master. Maintain consistency in your training sessions and be patient as your puppy learns this essential skill.

Clicker Training

I've found that one of the most effective ways to teach your puppy new behaviors is through clicker training! This science-based method uses positive reinforcement to help your pup learn new commands and tricks. It's a safe and fair way to teach them new things, and I highly recommend giving it a try.

Clicker training is based on the principles of operant conditioning, which involves teaching an animal to associate a specific behavior with a consequence, such as a reward or punishment. A clicker, a small handheld device, is used in clicker training to provide a consistent, unique sound that indicates the exact instant a desired behavior is achieved. The click is then followed by a reward, typically a small treat, to reinforce the behavior. The benefits of clicker training include:

- **Clear communication:** The clicker provides a clear and consistent signal to your puppy that they have performed the desired behavior correctly, reducing confusion and frustration during training.

- **Faster learning:** Because the clicker allows you to precisely mark the behavior you want to reinforce, your puppy can learn new skills more quickly and efficiently.

- **Positive reinforcement:** Clicker training is built on the foundation of positive reinforcement, which fosters a strong bond between you and your puppy, making training an enjoyable and rewarding experience for both of you.

To get started with clicker training, follow these steps:

1. **Charging the clicker:** Before using the clicker in training sessions, you must first "charge" it by creating a positive association between the click sound and a reward. To do this, simply click the clicker and immediately give your puppy a treat. Repeat this process several times over a few short sessions until your puppy shows excitement and anticipation when they hear the click.

2. **Capturing a behavior:** To teach your puppy a new behavior, wait for them to naturally perform the action (e.g., sitting or lying down) and then immediately click and treat. This process is called "capturing." Be patient and observant, as it may take some time for your puppy to perform the desired behavior on their own.

3. **Shaping a behavior:** For more complex behaviors, you can use a technique called "shaping," which involves rewarding small steps or approximations toward the final behavior. For example, if you're teaching your puppy to roll over, you might first click and treat when they lie down, then when they shift their weight to one side, and so on, until they complete the full roll.

4. **Adding a cue:** Once your puppy consistently performs the desired behavior in response to the clicker, you can introduce a verbal or visual cue (e.g., a hand signal or command) immediately before clicking and treating. Gradually phase out the clicker as your puppy begins to reliably respond to the cue alone.

5. **Proofing and generalizing:** To ensure your puppy can perform the behavior in various situations and environments, practice the skill in different locations and with varying levels of distraction. This process is known as "proofing" and "generalizing."

Teaching Key Commands

Training your puppy to understand and respond to key commands is an essential part of raising a well-mannered and well-adjusted dog. It takes time and patience to teach your furry friend the most important commands, but the effort is worth it in the end. In this chapter, you'll find practical examples and tips on how to teach your puppy the essential commands. With consistency and positive reinforcement, you and your canine companion can have a successful learning experience together.

Respond to Name

Teaching your puppy to respond to their name is the foundation of all future training. It helps to get your puppy's attention and focus, ensuring they are ready to learn.

1.   Choose a quiet, distraction-free environment to start.
2.   Say your puppy's name in a clear, upbeat tone.
3.   When your puppy looks at you, immediately praise and reward them with a treat.
4.   Repeat this process multiple times daily, gradually increasing the level of distractions around you.

Come

The "come" command is crucial for your puppy's safety and helps you maintain control in various situations.

1.   To begin, place yourself a short distance from your puppy.
2.   Call their name, followed by the command "come."
3.   When your puppy comes to you, praise and reward them with a treat.
4.   As your puppy becomes more adept at reliably following instructions, gradually increase the distance and other distractions.

Drop

The "drop" command teaches your puppy to release an object from their mouth, which is important for preventing possessive behavior and ensuring safety.

1.   Offer your puppy a toy or a chew they enjoy.
2.   When your puppy has the item in their mouth, present a high-value treat and say "drop."
3.   As your puppy releases the item to take the treat, praise them.
4.   Practice this command regularly, eventually transitioning to using the command without a treat.

Sit

The "sit" command is a basic obedience skill that helps your puppy develop self-control and good manners.

1. Hold a treat near your puppy's nose, then slowly move it up and back over their head.
2. Your puppy's bottom will drop naturally into a sitting position as their head follows the treat.
3. When your puppy sits, say "sit," praise them, and give them the treat.
4. Repeat this process multiple times daily, gradually fading out the use of the treat as a lure.

Wait

The "wait" command teaches your puppy to pause and remain in place, which is useful for controlling impulsive behaviors and promoting safety.

1. Ask your puppy to sit, then hold a treat in front of them and say "wait."
2. Wait a few seconds, then say "okay" and give your puppy the treat.
3. Gradually increase the duration of the "wait" command and introduce distractions.
4. Practice this command in various situations, such as waiting at doorways or before crossing the street.

Watch

The "watch" command teaches your puppy to make eye contact with you, which is important for maintaining focus during training and strengthening your bond.

1. Hold a treat near your eyes and say "watch."
2. When your puppy makes eye contact, praise and reward them with the treat.
3. Gradually increase the duration of eye contact and introduce distractions.
4. Transition to using the command without a treat, rewarding your puppy with praise and attention instead.

Stay

The "stay" command is essential for maintaining control over your puppy in various situations and helps to teach them self-control and patience.

1. Ask your puppy to sit or lie down.
2. Hold your hand out, palm facing your puppy, and say "stay."
3. Take a few steps back, then return to your puppy, and reward them with a treat and praise if they remained in place.
4. Gradually increase the distance and duration of the "stay" command, always rewarding your puppy for their success.
5. Introduce distractions and practice in different environments to strengthen your puppy's understanding of the command.

Lie Down

The "lie down" command is a useful obedience skill that can help your puppy remain calm and relaxed in various situations.

1. Have your puppy sit, then hold a treat near their nose and slowly lower it to the ground while saying "lie down."
2. As your puppy's head follows the treat, their body should naturally follow into a lying down position.
3. When your puppy lies down, praise them and give them the treat.
4. Practice this command regularly, gradually fading out the use of the treat as a lure.

Heel

The "heel" command teaches your puppy to walk politely by your side without pulling on the leash, ensuring enjoyable and controlled walks.

1. Begin by holding a treat in your hand and allowing your puppy to sniff it.
2. Say "heel" and start walking with the treat held at your side, just above your puppy's head.

3. As your puppy follows the treat and maintains a position close to your side, praise and reward them with the treat.
4. Gradually increase the duration of the "heel" command and introduce distractions.
5. Practice this command on walks, transitioning to using the command without a treat and rewarding your puppy with praise and attention instead.

Off

This command teaches your puppy to respect boundaries and refrain from jumping on people, furniture, or other surfaces.

1. When your puppy jumps up, calmly say "off" and turn your body away, avoiding eye contact.
2. Once your puppy's paws are back on the ground, praise and reward them with a treat.
3. Consistently reinforce this command, ensuring all family members and visitors follow the same training approach.
4. Practice this command in different environments and situations, reinforcing your puppy's understanding of the command.

The Importance of the Trainer's Nonverbal Language

When it comes to puppy training, it's not just about giving commands and getting responses. It's a conversation between you and your furry friend, where both verbal and nonverbal cues play an important role. As trainers, we sometimes forget how significant our body language and tone are in shaping the training experience for our puppies. By understanding the profound communication between you and your pet, you can create a more engaging and effective training experience.

The Significance of Body Language and Tone
In the animal kingdom, body language reigns supreme as the primary means of

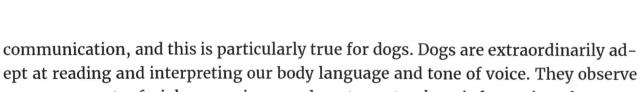

communication, and this is particularly true for dogs. Dogs are extraordinarily adept at reading and interpreting our body language and tone of voice. They observe our movements, facial expressions, and postures to glean information about our intentions, moods, and desires. For instance, standing tall with hands on the hips might be interpreted by a puppy as a display of dominance, while a soft, crouched posture could be seen as inviting play.

Similarly, our tone of voice carries a wealth of information that our puppies use to understand us better. A cheerful, high-pitched voice can signal praise and positivity, often exciting our puppies, while a deeper, stern tone might indicate a command that requires immediate attention.

Imagine teaching your puppy the "sit" command. By using a firm tone, clear verbal cue, and a hand signal pointing downwards, you're effectively conveying your expectation. When your puppy responds correctly, instantly switch to a lighter, praising tone, accompanied by rewarding body language such as gentle petting or giving a treat. This combination of tone and body language helps your puppy understand the difference between command and praise, making the training process more effective.

The Role of Consistency in Cues and Signals

Consistency is a pillar of effective puppy training. As much as dogs can interpret our nonverbal language, they thrive on consistency and routine. When it comes to training cues and signals, being consistent helps your puppy understand and respond to commands more quickly.

Let's say you're teaching your puppy to stay. If you use a flat palm facing downwards one day, a pointed finger the next, and a waving hand the day after that, your puppy could become confused about what you expect when you give the "stay" command. Sticking to one specific hand signal while verbalizing the command "stay" will reinforce the lesson in your puppy's mind, helping them associate that specific gesture and word with the desired behavior.

Consistency also extends to the timing of rewards and corrections. The immediate reinforcement of a behavior with a treat, praise, or a clicker (if you're clicker training), ensures that your puppy makes a clear connection between their action and the outcome. If there's a delay in giving the reward or if you inconsistently offer rewards, it can blur this connection and slow down the training process.

Decoding Your Dog's Body Language

One of the most fascinating aspects of the human-canine relationship is the ability to communicate across species lines. A vital part of this communication is understanding the body language of your dog. This unspoken dialogue is rich and varied, offering insight into your puppy's emotions, intentions, and needs. Learning to accurately interpret these signals is an essential skill for anyone involved in puppy training.

Understanding Common Signals and Postures

At the root of every difficulty you encounter with your furry friend lies a single word: "*misunderstanding*". The lack of a true bond of deep emotional understanding will render all your efforts to build a relationship based on respect, trust, and proper care futile. It is necessary to establish a fruitful and empathetic connection with your faithful four-legged companion from the very beginning, or else you will face behavioral and health problems, some of which may be severe and difficult to remedy, such as aggression, fear, anxiety, lack of vitality, and nutritional deficiencies.

It is therefore of fundamental importance that at this point in the guide, you correctly interpret some of its key signals that will open the doors to a unique bond with your best friend, ensuring their physical and psychological well-being. The correct understanding of certain specific situations is the key to what I have been able to achieve through my extensive experience as a trainer, even solving the most challenging cases.

With this practical manual, I have decided to share with you the proper interpretation of the messages your beloved friend wants to communicate, so that you can make yourself heard, keep your dog in excellent health, and create a unique and enviable bond between the two of you.

Here I explain my system of "*instant translation*" of your dog's language, which is so easy, accurate, and precise that it will feel like you're speaking their language to prevent all kind of issues and to provide an effective train.

▶ *Yawning*

Apparent Meaning: Yawning in dogs is often associated with tiredness or boredom. It is commonly perceived as a sign that the dog needs rest or is feeling sleepy.

Real Meaning: Yawning in dogs can serve as a stress signal or a way to diffuse tension. When a dog yawns in a situation that doesn't seem to warrant tiredness, it can be an indication of discomfort or anxiety. It is a form of communication that the dog uses to communicate their unease or to show submission to a perceived threat. Yawning in such contexts can signal the need for a break or a desire to distance themselves from the current situation.

▶ *Scratching*

Apparent Meaning: Scratching is typically seen as a natural behavior for dogs to relieve itchiness or discomfort caused by fleas, ticks, or other skin irritations. It is commonly associated with the dog needing relief from an external irritation.

Real Meaning: Scratching can also be a displacement behavior or a way for dogs to cope with stress or confusion. In situations that make them uncomfortable or uncertain, dogs may resort to scratching as a form of self-soothing. It is their way of redirecting their anxiety or frustration into a more manageable action. Paying attention to the context in which the scratching occurs can help determine if it is purely due to physical discomfort or if there are underlying emotional factors at play.

▶ *Nose Licking*

Apparent Meaning: Nose licking is often interpreted as a dog cleaning its snout or having leftover food or moisture on its face. It is commonly seen as a grooming behavior or a way to satisfy physical needs.

Real Meaning: Nose licking in dogs can be a sign of appeasement or anxiety. Dogs may lick their noses when they are feeling stressed, nervous, or uncomfortable in a social interaction. It is a way for them to communicate their non-threatening intentions and to signal submission or a desire to avoid conflict. Observing the context and accompanying body language can provide insights into the dog's emotional state and the reasons behind the nose licking behavior.

▶ *Tail Wagging*

Apparent Meaning: Tail wagging is often associated with happiness, excitement, or friendliness. It is commonly seen as a sign of a dog's positive emotions and a welcoming gesture.

Real Meaning: Tail wagging in dogs is a complex form of communication that can convey different messages depending on its intensity and accompanying body language. While a broad, loose wag generally indicates a positive emotional state, a stiff or low wag can signify caution, uncertainty, or even aggression. It is crucial to consider the overall context, including the dog's body posture, facial expressions, and the situation, to accurately interpret the meaning behind the tail wagging behavior.

▶ *Paw Lifting*

Apparent Meaning: Paw lifting is often perceived as a dog showing attention or requesting something, such as wanting to play or receive attention. It is commonly seen as an invitation for interaction.

Real Meaning: Paw lifting in dogs can serve multiple purposes beyond seeking attention. While it can indicate a desire for engagement, it can also be a sign of stress, uncertainty, or even discomfort. Dogs may lift their paws as a way to communicate their unease or to signal their submission in a potentially threatening situation. It is important to assess the overall body language and context to accurately interpret the message behind the paw lifting behavior.

▶ *Play Bow*

Apparent Meaning: When a dog lowers their front end while keeping their hind end elevated, it is commonly interpreted as an invitation to play.

Real Meaning: The play bow is indeed an invitation to play, indicating the dog's friendly and playful intentions. It is a clear signal that the dog is ready to engage in a playful interaction.

▶ *Raised Hackles*

Apparent Meaning: Raised hackles, the hair along a dog's back, are often seen as a sign of aggression or fear.

Real Meaning: While raised hackles can be associated with heightened arousal, they don't always indicate aggression or fear. In some cases, they may simply indicate excitement, alertness, or a dog's attempt to appear larger. It's essential to consider other body language cues to accurately interpret the dog's emotional state.

▶ *Tail Tucking*

Apparent Meaning: A tucked tail is commonly interpreted as a sign of fear or submission.

Real Meaning: While a tucked tail can indicate fear or submission, it is not always the case. Some dogs naturally have a tail that naturally curves or tucks. Additionally, a tucked tail can also signify nervousness, anxiety, or anticipation. It's crucial to assess the overall context and the dog's other body language cues to determine the precise meaning.

▶ *Ears Back*

Apparent Meaning: When a dog's ears are pulled back against their head, it is often thought to indicate fear or submission.

Real Meaning: Ears pulled back can indeed signal fear or submission, but they can also convey other emotions. Dogs may pull their ears back when they are feeling relaxed or content. In certain situations, such as during focused concentration or heightened arousal, the ears may naturally flatten or move back. It's necessary to consider the dog's body language as a whole to accurately interpret their emotional state.

Stiff Body Posture

Apparent Meaning: A dog with a stiff body posture is often perceived as aggressive or tense.

Real Meaning: While a stiff body posture can indicate aggression or tension, it can have other meanings as well. Some dogs naturally have a more rigid or upright stance. Additionally, a dog may become stiff when they are intensely focused or alert. It's important to consider the dog's overall behavior and other body language cues to determine the true meaning behind the stiffness.

Understanding these common dog signals requires considering the specific context, the dog's body language as a whole, and any accompanying behaviors to get a more accurate understanding of their true meaning. It is always beneficial to observe and assess multiple signals in combination to gain a comprehensive understanding of a dog's emotional state and intentions.

Responding Appropriately to Your Dog's Cues

Recognizing your puppy's body language is just the first step. Responding appropriately to their cues is equally important in fostering effective communication and mutual understanding.

- *Positive Signals:* When your puppy shows signs of comfort and happiness (like a relaxed body and a gently wagging tail), reinforce this positive behavior. Continue whatever action led to this response, be it petting, playing, or simply being in their presence.

- *Fear or Anxiety:* If your puppy displays signs of fear or anxiety, like flattened ears, a tucked tail, or a crouched body, it's important to identify and address the source of their discomfort. Avoid forceful confrontation and instead opt for gentle reassurance. In some cases, it may be helpful to remove your puppy from the stressful situation entirely.

- *Aggression or Dominance:* Signs of aggression or dominance, such as stiff posture, bared teeth, or a high, stiff tail wag, require careful handling. It's crucial not to respond with aggression of your own. Instead, maintain calm and assert your leadership through firm, confident commands.

By taking the time to understand your puppy's body language and respond appropriately, you're ensuring a healthier, happier relationship with your pet. This mutual understanding not only deepens your bond but also makes training sessions more effective and enjoyable for both of you. Remember, every dog is unique, so while these general interpretations offer a starting point, getting to know your specific pet's behaviors is crucial to truly understand their communication.

Socializing an Older Dog

In the realm of canine companionship, it's a common misconception that only puppies are capable of being socialized. While it's true that a puppy's formative months present a golden opportunity for socialization, it's never too late to introduce an older dog to new experiences. With patience, consistency, and compassion, you can socialize an adult dog and enhance their quality of life exponentially. In this chapter, we'll explore the challenges and benefits associated with socializing an older dog, along with a trove of practical tips for successful socialization.

The Challenges and Benefits
Socializing an older dog might present its unique set of challenges, but the rewards it reaps are manifold.

- **Challenges:** Older dogs may have ingrained behaviors, fears, or past traumas that make them resistant to new experiences. They may exhibit signs of fear or aggression in unfamiliar situations or when introduced to new people or animals.

- **Benefits:** Successfully socializing an older dog can significantly enhance their happiness and overall wellbeing. A well-socialized dog will be less likely to exhibit fear or aggression, more comfortable in different settings, and generally more relaxed and content.

Practical Tips for Successful Socialization
While each dog is unique and there's no one-size-fits-all approach, these general strategies can guide you in socializing an older dog:

- *Start Slow:* With an older dog, it's especially important to introduce new experiences gradually. Start by exposing your dog to new people, animals, and environments in a controlled and calm manner. Remember, it's crucial to keep these encounters positive.

- *Reward Good Behavior:* Positive reinforcement is key in socializing older dogs. Whenever your dog responds well to a new experience, reward them with treats, praise, or petting. This will help them associate new experiences with positive outcomes.

- *Use Desensitization Techniques:* If your dog is particularly fearful of specific stimuli, gradual desensitization can be very effective. This involves introducing the fear-inducing stimuli at a low intensity and gradually increasing the intensity over time, always paired with positive reinforcement.

- *Patience is Key:* Patience is perhaps the most important ingredient in this process. Changes won't happen overnight, and there may be setbacks along the way. Remember to celebrate small victories and not to push your dog too far, too fast.

Identifying Your Dog's Potential Service Tasks

Dogs are remarkable creatures not only for their companionship but also for their capacity to assist humans in countless ways. A well-trained service dog can drastically improve the quality of life for individuals living with physical, psychological, or psychiatric disabilities. However, not all dogs are suitable for all types of service roles, and it's vital to assess your pet's aptitude and inclinations carefully. This chapter will explore the realms of psychiatric, medical, and mobility assistance, and will guide you through assessing your dog's suitability for these roles and understanding the training requirements involved.

Psychiatric Assistance: Psychiatric Service Dogs (PSDs) are trained to support individuals with psychiatric conditions like PTSD, anxiety disorders, or depression. These dogs might perform tasks like providing a grounding presence during a panic attack, reminding their handler to take medication, or interrupting self-harming behaviors. To excel in this role, a dog should exhibit strong emotional attunement and a calm demeanor. Breeds known for their sensitivity and intelligence, like Labrador Retrievers or Golden Retrievers, can often thrive in these positions. However, any breed can serve as a PSD, provided they demonstrate the right attributes.

Medical Assistance: Medical Alert Dogs (MADs) are trained to assist individuals with various medical conditions like diabetes, seizures, or severe allergies. These dogs can detect changes in their handler's physiological state—like blood sugar fluctuations or the onset of a seizure—and respond accordingly. A strong sense of smell and keen observant nature are paramount attributes for a MAD. Again, while some breeds may be more inclined towards this type of work—like German Shepherds or Border Collies—suitability heavily depends on the individual dog's characteristics.

Mobility Assistance: Mobility Service Dogs assist individuals with physical disabilities or mobility issues. These dogs may help with tasks like opening doors, retrieving items, or even providing physical support for balance. For this role, physical strength and stamina are crucial. Larger breeds like Newfoundlanders or Saint Bernards are often chosen for this type of work due to their size and power. However, smaller dogs can also be mobility aids, depending on the specific needs of the handler.

Assessing Suitability and Training Requirements: Assessing your dog's potential for service work involves observing their temperament, physical capabilities, and overall health. It's essential to consult with a professional trainer or a service dog organization for a thorough evaluation. Training a service dog is a complex, time-consuming process that should only be carried out by professionals or under professional guidance. It requires the dog to master basic obedience, public access manners, and specific task training related to the handler's needs.

In summary, while the journey to becoming a service dog is rigorous, the impact these dogs can have on the lives of their handlers is profoundly transformative. With the correct training and a lot of love and patience, these amazing animals can truly embody the adage "man's best friend."

The Lifelong Impact of Early Training and Socialization

As we close this chapter on puppy training, it is important to reiterate the profound lifelong impact that early training and socialization can have on your dog. The lessons learned, habits formed, and experiences gathered during these formative weeks and months serve as the foundation for your puppy's future behavior, well-being, and overall quality of life. Training and socializing your puppy from an early age provides a solid groundwork for positive behavior. It helps shape a dog that is obedient, calm, and balanced. It also minimizes potential issues such as aggression, anxiety, or excessive fearfulness. Early training sets the stage for your dog to grow into a well-mannered, sociable, and friendly adult that can easily integrate into various social situations, whether that involves interacting with other animals, adapting to new environments, or being around different people.

Socialization is integral to your puppy's development, enabling them to understand and navigate the world around them. Exposing your puppy to a variety of experiences helps to build their confidence, reduce fear and anxiety, and enhance their ability to handle new situations. This exposure should encompass different sights, sounds, smells, people, and other animals.

The benefits of early training and socialization also extend to you as a dog owner. Training is a bonding experience that builds trust, mutual respect, and a deep connection between you and your dog. It allows you to better understand your dog's behavior, facilitating easier communication and a more harmonious cohabitation. Moreover, a well-trained and socialized dog is generally easier to manage, reducing potential stress and allowing you to fully enjoy the companionship of your furry friend. However, it's crucial to remember that training and socialization are not one-time events but ongoing processes. Your dog will continue learning throughout their life, and consistently reinforcing good behavior is key to maintaining the gains achieved during early training. Investing time and effort into properly training and socializing your puppy from the start will pay dividends throughout your dog's life. It will contribute to the creation of a loving, trustful, and long-lasting relationship between you and your dog, enhancing both your lives for many years to come. Remember, the goal is not to cultivate a perfect dog but to nurture a dog that is perfect for you, and early training and socialization is a significant step in this direction.

   In the next step I cover topics related to the health and wellbeing of your dog. I discuss proper nutrition, exercise, grooming, socialization, mental stimulation, and common health issues. Throughout this section, I emphasize the importance of prioritizing your dog's physical and emotional health to ensure a long, fulfilling life by your side.

PART IV

HEALTH AND WELLBEING

"Dogs are wise. They crawl away into a quiet corner and lick their wounds and do not rejoin the world until they are whole once more."
—Agatha Christie

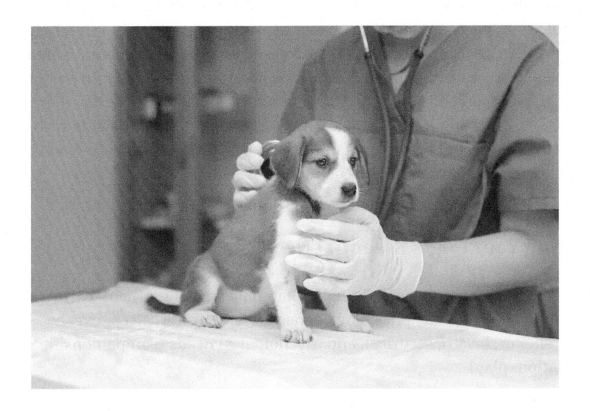

Imagine being in a world where you can't verbally express your needs, fears, or discomforts. A world where you entirely rely on others to interpret your subtle cues, meet your needs, and ensure your well-being. This is the world your dog inhabits. Therefore, understanding your puppy's perspective is the cornerstone of responsible and successful dog ownership.

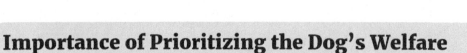

Importance of Prioritizing the Dog's Welfare

Owning a dog is a commitment that extends far beyond providing food and shelter. It's about ensuring the overall welfare of your four-legged friend. But what does prioritizing a dog's welfare mean? Primarily, it's recognizing that your dog is a living being with feelings and needs, not a mere accessory or toy. Dogs are capable of experiencing a spectrum of emotions, including joy, sadness, fear, and love. Respecting these emotions is crucial to their psychological well-being.

Your dog's welfare is directly linked to their quality of life. A dog who's well cared for will be physically healthy, emotionally balanced, and exhibit appropriate behavior. Prioritizing your dog's welfare involves meeting their physical needs like nutrition, exercise, healthcare, and grooming. But equally important is catering to their psychological needs, such as companionship, mental stimulation, and a sense of security. Think of Bella, a Golden Retriever, who thrives on companionship and physical activity. If her family neglects her need for exercise and interaction, Bella might resort to destructive behaviors, like chewing furniture or excessive barking, out of boredom or anxiety. It's not that Bella is a 'bad dog', but rather her essential needs are not being met.

Meeting Your Dog's Essential Needs

Every dog, like humans, has basic needs that must be met for them to live a healthy, happy life. These include physiological needs (food, water, sleep, exercise), safety needs (shelter, health, security), and psychological needs (companionship, mental stimulation, play).

- **Physiological Needs:** Proper nutrition is vital for your dog's health. Choosing a diet that's appropriate for your dog's age, breed, and health status is crucial. Regular exercise keeps your dog physically fit and helps burn off excess energy, reducing behavioral problems. Always ensure your dog has access to clean drinking water.

- **Safety Needs:** Regular vet checks and timely vaccinations are essential to prevent diseases and catch any potential health issues early. Providing a safe, comfortable space for your dog to rest and sleep is also part of meeting their safety needs.

- **Psychological Needs:** Dogs are social animals and need companionship. Spending quality time with your dog, providing mental stimulation (through toys, training, etc.), and ensuring they have opportunities for play are crucial to their mental well-being.

For example, Max, a Border Collie, has a high need for mental and physical stimulation. To meet these needs, his family includes him in their daily activities, provides puzzle toys, and organizes regular agility training. Remember, meeting your dog's essential needs requires understanding their unique characteristics and preferences. A dog who feels loved, secure, and fulfilled is more likely to exhibit good behavior and be a joy to live with. By embracing your dog's perspective, you not only ensure their welfare but also strengthen the bond you share with your furry friend.

Food and Nutrition

Food plays a vital role in your puppy's life. It fuels their growth, keeps their fur glossy, strengthens their immune system, and provides the energy they need for their everyday antics. However, proper nutrition involves more than just feeding your puppy. It requires a deep understanding of their nutritional needs, recognizing the right and wrong foods, selecting appropriate rewards, and exploring the option of homemade food.

Essentials of Dog Nutrition

Just as humans do, dogs require a balanced diet for optimal health. But what does a balanced diet for a dog entail? Primarily, it includes proteins, carbohydrates, fats, vitamins, and minerals, each serving its purpose. Proteins are vital for tissue repair and muscle growth. They're especially important for puppies who are still growing. Carbohydrates, while not a must-have in a dog's diet, provide them with energy and help keep the gut healthy. Fats are essential for the absorption of certain vitamins and also serve as a great energy source. Lastly, vitamins and minerals are necessary for various metabolic reactions in the body. For instance, a puppy like Ollie, a growing Labrador, would require a diet high in protein to support his rapid growth and high energy levels.

Here's a list explaining the nutritional deficiencies that may underlie each of the mentioned dog problems, along with their associated issues:

Digestive Problems:
Nutritional Deficiency: Insufficient dietary fiber
Associated Issues: Poor digestion, irregular bowel movements, and discomfort

Stools that are too soft or too hard:
Nutritional Deficiency: Imbalance in fiber intake or inadequate hydration
Associated Issues: Loose, watery stools (diarrhea) or dry, hard stools (constipation)

Constipation:
Nutritional Deficiency: Lack of dietary fiber and hydration
Associated Issues: Difficulty in passing stools, straining, and infrequent bowel movements

Diarrhea:
Nutritional Deficiency: Imbalance in fiber intake, excessive fat, or poor-quality ingredients
Associated Issues: Frequent, loose, and watery stools

Flatulence:
Nutritional Deficiency: Poor digestion of certain nutrients (e.g., carbohydrates)
Associated Issues: Excessive gas production, bloating, and discomfort

Foul Smelling Stools:
Nutritional Deficiency: Poor digestion and absorption of nutrients
Associated Issues: Offensive odor in the stools, which may indicate malabsorption or imbalanced gut bacteria

Obesity:
Nutritional Deficiency: Excessive calorie intake and inadequate exercise
Associated Issues: Weight gain, reduced mobility, and increased risk of various health problems

Itching:
Nutritional Deficiency: Lack of essential fatty acids or imbalanced omega-6 to omega-3 ratio
Associated Issues: Skin irritation, dryness, and itching due to compromised skin health

Shaggy and Matted Fur:
Nutritional Deficiency: Inadequate protein, essential fatty acids, and overall nutrient imbalance
Associated Issues: Dull, dry, and tangled fur, prone to matting and poor coat quality

Bone-Articular Problems:
Nutritional Deficiency: Lack of essential nutrients like calcium, phosphorus, and vitamin D
Associated Issues: Weakened bones, joint problems, and increased risk of fractures or developmental issues

It's important to note that while these deficiencies can contribute to the mentioned problems, they may not be the sole cause. Other factors such as underlying health conditions, environmental factors, and genetics can also play a role. Consulting with a veterinarian is crucial for accurate diagnosis and tailored nutritional recommendations to address specific dog problems.

Choosing the Right Dog Foods

With countless dog food brands available, choosing the right one can be overwhelming. Look for foods that meet the standards set by the Association of American Feed Control Officials (AAFCO). The food label should indicate that it's complete and balanced, which means it should have all the necessary nutrients.

Select the food suitable for your dog's life stage (puppy, adult, or senior) and size (small breed or large breed). For instance, smaller breeds like Yorkshire Terriers require different nutrition than larger breeds like Great Danes.

Understanding Toxic Foods

While dogs may be eager to eat everything they come across, not all foods are safe for them. Certain foods can be toxic to dogs, including chocolate, avocado, grapes, raisins, onions, garlic, salt, xylitol (a common sweetener), and alcohol. Make sure these items are out of your dog's reach and that all family members understand the dangers of these foods. If your dog ingests any of these, seek veterinary attention immediately.

Choosing Suitable Rewards

Treats are a great way to reward your puppy during training sessions, but choosing the right treats is key. They should be small (so your puppy doesn't get full quickly) and healthy. Avoid treats high in sugar or artificial ingredients. Many dogs love baby carrots, apples (without seeds), or a piece of boiled chicken as a treat. However, remember that treats should only constitute about 10% of your dog's daily caloric intake.

Homemade Food Options and Precautions

Preparing your dog's meals at home gives you control over what goes into their diet. Keep in mind that certain foods are great for dogs, like lean meats, certain fruits and vegetables, and whole grains. But some, like avocado, raw bread dough, and foods high in salt and spices, can be harmful. Taking charge of your dog's diet can feel daunting with all the factors to consider, but with your vet's guidance and your growing understanding of your dog's nutritional needs, it's a challenge that can enhance your dog's health and lifespan. Proper nutrition is one of the many ways you express your love and care for your four-legged family member.

Canine Superfoods: The Perfect Meal Plan

Virtually all traditional dog foods, including kibble, canned food, or homemade meals, lack at least one of the three essential nutrients necessary for optimal health in dogs.

Firstly, these foods lack the ten essential amino acids that serve as the "building blocks" for a dog's body, particularly their vital organs.

Secondly, they do not provide essential probiotics and prebiotics, which are vital for regulating the digestive system, facilitating nutrient absorption, and strengthening the immune system.

Lastly, these foods fail to supply the essential minerals, such as copper, zinc, and manganese, which regulate various aspects of a dog's health, including teeth, skin and coat quality, and overall energy levels.

Scientific evidence confirms that traditional kibble diets and homemade food almost always fall short in providing these essential nutrients for dogs.

Here is a list of **seven easy ingredients** that you may already have in your home, unknowingly, and that are beneficial for dogs of all breeds, sizes, and ages.

Regularly incorporating these foods, which you may have never considered or received recommendations for, can have multiple benefits. These include soothing irritated and itchy skin, restoring energy levels, enhancing fur and coat shine, regulating digestion, boosting immunity, improving heart health, enhancing brain function, and more.

1. **"Nooch"** also known as nutritional yeast, is a complete protein source that contains all ten essential amino acids needed by dogs.

2. **Enterococcus faecium** is a probiotic that aids in regulating digestion.

3. **Fructo-oligosaccharides (FOS)** and **mannan-oligosaccharides (MOS)** help maintain a healthy balance of good and bad bacteria in the gut. These prebiotics can be found in certain fruits and vegetables such as bananas, apples, and carrots. You can offer small amounts of these foods as treats or incorporate them into your dog's homemade meals.

4. **Five essential minerals:** copper, iron, zinc, manganese, and iodine, which enhance immunity, skin health, energy levels, and more. These minerals can be found in various natural food sources. For example, copper can be obtained from liver, iron from lean meats like beef or chicken, zinc from seafood such as fish or oysters, manganese from leafy greens, and iodine from seaweed or fish.

5. **Pumpkin** aids in digestion regulation, acts as an additional prebiotic, and contains vitamins A, C, and E. You can offer canned, unsweetened pumpkin puree as a source of fiber, vitamins A, C, and E, and as an additional prebiotic to regulate digestion. Make sure it does not contain added sugars or spices.

6. **Curcumin** helps alleviate joint stiffness and soothes itchy skin. Turmeric is a natural source of curcumin. You can find turmeric powder and add a small amount to your dog's food.

7. **Vitamins E, B2,** and **B12** increase energy levels and enhance brain function in dogs. These vitamins can be found in various food sources. Vitamin E can be obtained from foods like almonds, sunflower seeds, and spinach. Vitamin B2 (riboflavin) can be found in eggs, lean meats, and dairy products. Vitamin B12 is primarily found in animal-based products such as liver, fish, and eggs.

By incorporating these foods into your dog's diet, you can provide them with the necessary nutrients to support their overall well-being. However, it's always advisable to consult with a veterinarian for specific dietary recommendations tailored to your dog's individual needs.

Here is a comprehensive list of **4 easy and healthy superfoods** for dogs, along with their benefits:

Carrots
Benefits: Carrots are high in fiber and low in calories, making them great for weight management. They are also a good source of vitamins A and K, which promote healthy vision and blood clotting.

Apples

Benefits: Apples are packed with vitamins A and C, as well as fiber. They promote healthy digestion and can freshen your dog's breath. Remember to remove the seeds and core before feeding them to your dog.

Eggs

Benefits: Eggs are an excellent source of protein, providing essential amino acids for muscle growth and repair. They also contain vitamins A, D, E, and various B vitamins. Make sure eggs are fully cooked before feeding them to your dog.

Pumpkin

Benefits: Pumpkin is rich in fiber and can help regulate your dog's digestive system. It also contains beta-carotene, which supports eye health, and antioxidants that promote overall well-being.

Now, here's **the perfect homemade meal plan** that includes these *superfoods* for each of the three dog categories:

1. *Small Breed Adult Dog (For example: Chihuahua)*

Breakfast
- Scrambled eggs (1 egg)
- Steamed carrots (1/4 cup)

Lunch
- Cooked chicken breast (1/4 cup)
- Apple slices (1/4 cup)
-

Dinner
- Baked pumpkin cubes (1/4 cup)
- Ground turkey (1/4 cup)

2. Large Breed Puppy (For example: Labrador Retriever)

Breakfast
- Hard-boiled egg (1/2 egg)
- Steamed carrots (1/4 cup)

Lunch
- Cooked lean beef (1/4 cup)
- Apple slices (1/4 cup)

Dinner
- Baked pumpkin cubes (1/4 cup)
- Cooked salmon (1/4 cup)

3. Senior Dog (For example: German Shepherd)

Breakfast
- Scrambled egg whites (2 egg whites)
- Steamed carrots (1/4 cup)

Lunch
- Cooked turkey (1/4 cup)
- Apple slices (1/4 cup)

Dinner
- Baked pumpkin cubes (1/4 cup)
- Cooked white fish (1/4 cup)

Remember to adjust portion sizes according to your dog's specific needs and consult with your veterinarian for any dietary concerns or allergies.

Remember that in order to develop a balanced, healthy food plan for your 4-legged friend, you need to assess his or her lifestyle and daily activity level. This is why is I want to share with you **my Secret Workbook** comprehensive of a

Weekly Meal Plan that with my long experience as a trainer I have properly incorporated within the Weekly Exercises Plan.

You can easily download it here (Weekly Program-Boost Phase).

Remember that according to your personal time requirements you can repeat this weekly program as you like, varying the daily combinations according to your preferences and the specific health status of your dog.

Alternative Meal Plan

Designing a meal plan for your dog with high quality dried dog food can be an excellent alternative to ensure they get a balanced diet, which is tailored to their specific needs. Keep in mind that these are examples and any changes in your dog's diet should be done under the supervision of your trusted Vet. Your dog's breed, size, age, weight, activity level, and health status all factor into determining the right diet for them. Here are example meal plans for three different types of dogs: a small breed adult, a large breed puppy, and a senior dog.

1. Small Breed Adult Dog

Adult small breeds have fast metabolisms and usually require a diet high in quality protein and fat.

Breakfast
- high-quality small breed dry dog food (1/4 cup)
- A tablespoon of wet food (for added hydration and flavor)

Lunch
- high-quality small breed dry dog food (1/4 cup)

Dinner
- high-quality small breed dry dog food (1/4 cup)
- A teaspoon of cooked lean chicken or turkey for added protein

2. *Large Breed Puppy*

Large breed puppies like Labradors have specific dietary needs to support their rapid growth and prevent joint health issues later in life.

Breakfast
- 1 cup of large breed puppy dry food
- A tablespoon of wet puppy food (for added hydration and flavor)

Lunch
- 1 cup of large breed puppy dry food
- A few pieces of cooked vegetables like sweet potatoes or carrots

Dinner
- 1 cup of large breed puppy dry food
- A tablespoon of wet puppy food
- A teaspoon of fish oil for added omega-3 and omega-6 fatty acids

3. *Senior Dog*

Senior dogs may have decreased activity levels and potential health issues, such as arthritis or obesity, which necessitate a different diet.

Breakfast
- 3/4 cup of senior-specific dry dog food
- A tablespoon of wet senior dog food for added hydration and flavor

Lunch:
- 1/4 cup of cooked lean protein (like chicken or turkey)

Dinner
- 3/4 cup of senior-specific dry dog food
- A tablespoon of wet senior dog food
- A sprinkle of a joint supplement recommended by your vet, if necessary

Please note: Always ensure your dog has access to fresh, clean water throughout the day. It's an essential part of their diet. Also, these meal plans are just starting points and the portions may need to be adjusted based on your dog's individual energy needs.

Exercise and Mental Stimulation

Exercise and mental stimulation are two key components of a dog's overall well-being. They are as integral to a dog's health as a balanced diet, vaccinations, and regular check-ups.

Importance of Regular Physical Exercise

Physical exercise plays a significant role in maintaining your dog's health. It not only keeps your dog's weight in check but also helps to prevent many health issues such as heart disease, arthritis, and depression. Furthermore, it aids in digestion and promotes healthier sleep patterns. Regular exercise also provides an opportunity for your dog to explore their environment, which can significantly contribute to their emotional wellbeing.

For example, a daily walk is essential for all dogs, regardless of their breed, size, or age. It allows them to satisfy their instinct to roam and sniff out new smells, an activity that offers mental stimulation as well as physical exercise.

Activities for Promoting Physical Health

A variety of physical activities can help keep your dog fit. Fetching games promote running and sprinting, while tug-of-war can provide muscle-building resistance. Swimming is another excellent, low-impact exercise for dogs, especially in the hot summer months. For younger or more energetic dogs, agility training can be an exciting way to get them moving while also strengthening their coordination and focus.

For instance, setting up an agility course in your backyard can provide an exciting challenge for your dog. Start with basic obstacles such as hoops and hurdles, and as your dog becomes more comfortable, you can introduce more complex challenges.

Mental Stimulation and Games for Cognitive Health

Just as the body needs exercise to stay healthy, the mind requires stimulation to stay sharp. Mental stimulation can help prevent cognitive decline, reduce boredom, and mitigate behavior problems. Puzzles, interactive games, and training exercises can all serve to challenge your dog mentally. One practical example of a mentally stimulating game is a food puzzle. These toys, filled with treats or kibble, require your dog to solve a problem to get their reward, engaging their problem-solving skills and focus.

In the last 20 years of my life, I have developed an exceptional dog training program. This comprehensive program equips you with all the knowledge and tools needed to raise an extraordinary canine companion from puppyhood to adulthood. It focuses on teaching proper behavior, obedience, and the foundations of a healthy lifestyle, ensuring that you raise the best dog ever.

I want to offer you my exclusive program *"Well-Behaved Companion Program"* as a **FREE BONUS**. You can easily and quickly download it with the **QR code** that you will find inside the paperback version of the book – Go at the end of the book to download the free bonuses, and start with easy and effective training sessions for your furry beloved companion!

Building Empathy through Shared Activities

Shared activities help strengthen the bond between you and your dog, fostering a deeper understanding and empathy. These can range from structured activities like training sessions or agility courses to more relaxed interactions like grooming or even simply relaxing together. In practice, regular grooming sessions not only help keep your dog clean and healthy but also provide an opportunity for quiet, gentle interaction. During these times, speak softly to your dog, praising them for their patience and good behavior, and always end the grooming session with a treat or a favorite game. This positive reinforcement will not only make future grooming easier but will also strengthen the empathetic bond between you and your dog.

Remember, maintaining a good balance of both physical and mental activities is key to ensuring your dog's overall health and happiness. The most important thing is to stay engaged and responsive to your dog's needs as they change over time.

House Training

House training is an essential part of rearing a puppy or welcoming an older dog into your home. While it can be a challenging period, the patience and consistent effort invested in this process yield invaluable rewards, creating a comfortable living space for both you and your canine companion.

Basics of House Training

House training begins with understanding your dog's needs and learning to anticipate their toilet habits. This involves recognizing the signs that your dog needs to eliminate, such as sniffing around, circling, whining, or trying to get your attention. You'll also need to familiarize yourself with your dog's natural schedule. Puppies, for instance, usually need to go out immediately after waking up, after eating, and after active play. This translates into many trips outdoors each day. Older dogs, on the other hand, can generally hold it longer and may require fewer outings. For instance, when you bring home a puppy, start by taking them out every hour or two. This not only prevents accidents but also provides plenty of opportunities for them to get it right and earn praise.

Setting a Routine

Consistency is crucial in-house training. Try to maintain a regular feeding schedule and limit water intake before bedtime to minimize night-time accidents. Establish a designated outdoor spot for elimination, leading your dog there each time. This consistency helps your dog understand where they should go. For instance, suppose you're training a new puppy named Bella. Try to feed Bella at the same times each day and take her out immediately afterwards. Also, take her to the same spot in your yard each time, using a cue word like "potty" to help her associate the area with the action.

Fun house games

 ### Game 1: Hide and Seek

Instructions: Hide in a different area of the house and call your dog's name. Encourage them to find you by using a happy and excited tone. When your dog finds you, reward them with praise and treats.

Benefits: This game promotes mental stimulation, as your dog uses their senses to locate you. It strengthens the bond between you and your dog, enhances their problem-solving skills, and builds trust and confidence.

Game 2: Treasure Hunt

Instructions: Hide small treats or toys around the house and encourage your dog to find them using their sense of smell. Start with easy hiding spots and gradually increase the difficulty level.

Benefits: This game taps into your dog's natural scavenging instincts and strengthens their scent detection abilities. It provides mental stimulation, engages their problem-solving skills, and encourages independent thinking.

Game 3: Tug of War

Instructions: Use a sturdy rope or tug toy and engage in a gentle game of tug with your dog. Remember to establish rules and boundaries, such as letting go of the toy when asked, to maintain control during play.

Benefits: Tug of War is an interactive and energetic game that allows you to bond with your dog while promoting physical exercise. It helps release pent-up energy, strengthens jaw muscles, and improves impulse control when played with rules in place.

Game 4: Simon Says

Instructions: Use basic obedience commands such as "sit," "lie down," or "stay" and play a modified version of Simon Says with your dog. Reward them with treats and praise for following the correct commands.

Benefits: This game reinforces obedience training, improves your dog's responsiveness to commands, and deepens the communication between you and your dog. It also enhances their focus, attention, and impulse control.

Game 5: Shell Game

Instructions: Gather three cups or containers and place a treat under one of them. Shuffle the cups and encourage your dog to find the cup with the treat. Reward them when they choose the correct cup.

Benefits: The Shell Game stimulates your dog's problem-solving abilities and strengthens their cognitive skills. It promotes focus, memory, and concentration while providing a fun and engaging way to interact with your dog.

Find the full list of brain games in my exclusive program "*Well-Behaved Companion Program*" that you can easily download it with the **QR code at the end of this book**.

Medications and Vet Care

In addition to the joys and companionship that come with owning a dog, it also comes with responsibilities. One of these is ensuring their health and well-being through regular veterinary care and, when necessary, medication administration. Understanding common health issues and recognizing signs that your dog needs professional medical attention can be a lifesaver.

Recognizing Common Health Issues

Dogs, like humans, are prone to a variety of health issues. Some common ones include flea and tick infestations, allergies, digestive issues, and ear infections. Being aware of these common problems can help you take preventive measures and recognize symptoms early on. For example, if your dog Bella starts scratching excessively, you might suspect a flea infestation. An over-the-counter flea medication might suffice, but in severe cases, you may need a stronger prescription treatment from the vet.

Signs Your Dog Needs to See a Vet

While minor issues can often be handled at home, certain signs warrant an immediate trip to the vet. These include sudden changes in behavior, drastic weight loss or gain, lethargy, loss of appetite, vomiting, diarrhea, difficulty urinating,

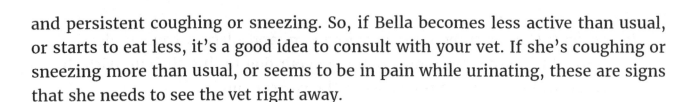
and persistent coughing or sneezing. So, if Bella becomes less active than usual, or starts to eat less, it's a good idea to consult with your vet. If she's coughing or sneezing more than usual, or seems to be in pain while urinating, these are signs that she needs to see the vet right away.

Basics of Administering Medications

Administering medication to a dog can be a daunting task, especially if they are uncooperative. Whether you're administering an oral medication, an ear drop, or a topical treatment, it's important to stay calm and be patient. For oral medications, using a treat-dispensing toy or wrapping the pill in a tasty treat can be helpful. If Bella needs to take a pill, you might try wrapping it in a slice of deli meat or inserting it into a soft treat specifically designed for hiding medication. If she's reluctant, you may need to gently open her mouth and place the pill in the back of her throat, then reward her with a treat afterward.

Administering topical medications or ear drops often requires a calm and gentle approach. It might be helpful to have a second person hold Bella while you apply the medicine. Whether your dog's healthcare routine involves prevention, treatment, or a bit of both, understanding common health issues, recognizing when professional help is needed, and knowing how to administer medications are key aspects of ensuring your dog's overall well-being. Always remember that your vet is your best resource when it comes to your dog's health.

Common Health Problems & Treatments

In the world of dog ownership, health and wellbeing extend far beyond the basics of food, water, and regular walks. It encompasses a broad scope of care that requires vigilant monitoring and a proactive approach towards potential health issues. It's essential to understand that our canine companions depend entirely on us to ensure their physical, mental, and emotional health.

This compendium delves into common health concerns, from dental issues and behavioral changes to obesity and weight management. We'll explore symptoms, potential causes, and suitable treatments, always stressing that the information presented here is not a substitute for professional veterinary advice. This knowledge aims to equip you with the necessary tools to be proactive about your dog's health, ensuring they live a long, active, and contented life by your side.

Please remember that it's essential to consult with a vet before implementing any treatments. These outlines are meant to provide an initial understanding, and individual treatment may vary depending on the specific case and the dog's overall health condition.

I. Digestive Issues

Digestive issues can often manifest as symptoms like vomiting, diarrhea, loss of appetite, or weight loss. These can be caused by a variety of factors, including dietary indiscretion (eating something they shouldn't have), parasites, infections, and allergies. Treatment usually involves identifying and eliminating the cause, modifying the diet, and administering medications such as antibiotics, antiparasitic, or antiemetics. Hydration support can also be crucial in these cases.

II. Skin Issues (Allergies, Infections, Parasites)

Skin issues are commonly identified through excessive scratching or licking, hair loss, redness and inflammation, or bumps, lesions, or rashes. Causes can range from fleas or ticks, bacterial or fungal infections, to allergies (food or environmental). Treatment typically includes identifying and eliminating the cause, using topical treatments, and providing oral medications like antihistamines, antibiotics, or steroids. Parasite prevention is also a crucial aspect of treatment.

III. Respiratory Issues

Respiratory issues can be indicated through symptoms like coughing, sneezing, difficulty breathing, or nasal discharge. Infections (bacterial, viral), allergies, and a foreign body in the respiratory tract are some of the potential causes. Treatment usually involves identifying and eliminating the cause, providing antibiotics for

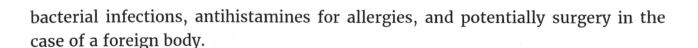

bacterial infections, antihistamines for allergies, and potentially surgery in the case of a foreign body.

IV. Musculoskeletal Issues

Symptoms of musculoskeletal issues include limping or difficulty moving, stiffness or weakness, and pain when touched. These can be caused by injuries, arthritis, or congenital or developmental disorders. Treatment usually revolves around identifying and eliminating the cause, managing the pain with NSAIDs or steroids, utilizing physical therapy, and possibly surgery.

V. Dental Issues

Dental issues are a common yet often overlooked aspect of a dog's health. Bad breath, difficulty chewing, excessive drooling, or noticeable tartar and plaque buildup are signs of potential oral health problems. Causes can range from lack of dental hygiene leading to periodontal disease, broken or infected teeth, or even oral tumors. Treatments usually involve professional teeth cleaning by a vet, potential tooth extractions for severely diseased teeth, and implementing a routine dental care regimen at home.

VI. Behavioral Changes

Changes in behavior can often signify health problems. Symptoms may include changes in eating or sleeping habits, lethargy, unexplained aggression, or increased anxiety. The causes of behavioral changes are varied and can range from physical health problems (pain, illness) to mental health issues (anxiety, cognitive dysfunction in older dogs). Treatment generally requires identifying the underlying cause and addressing it, which may involve medical treatment, behavioral therapy, or modifications to the dog's environment or routine.

VII. Obesity and Weight Management Issues

Obesity is a growing issue in pets and can lead to severe health problems, including diabetes, arthritis, and heart disease. Signs of obesity include difficulty moving, shortness of breath, and noticeable weight gain. The cause is usually a combination of overfeeding and lack of sufficient exercise. Treatment involves a carefully controlled diet and an appropriate exercise regime, sometimes along with vet-prescribed medication to address any underlying conditions contributing to the weight gain.

Dental Hygiene

Canine dental hygiene is an essential aspect of overall dog health that, unfortunately, is often relegated to the back burner. A solid understanding of the importance of dental hygiene, routine dental care procedures, and the ability to recognize dental health issues can significantly enhance your pup's quality of life and longevity.

Similar to human dental care, a dog's dental hygiene has far-reaching effects on its overall health. A dog's mouth is a gateway to its body. When left unattended, the buildup of bacteria in the mouth can lead to painful and detrimental conditions such as periodontal disease, tooth loss, bone loss, and systemic infections that can extend to vital organs like the heart, liver, and kidneys. For these reasons, maintaining your dog's dental hygiene is not merely about ensuring a bright canine smile but is fundamentally about safeguarding its overall health and wellness.

For routine dental care at home, it's ideal to brush your dog's teeth daily. The act of brushing removes the soft plaque that hardens and turns into tartar. Tartar below the gumline can only be removed professionally, and if left untreated, it can lead to infections that may enter the bloodstream. Start brushing your dog's teeth at a young age to acclimatize them to this routine. Utilize dog-specific toothpaste, as it is formulated to be safe for dogs to ingest, unlike human toothpaste.

Moreover, the market offers a plethora of dental hygiene products for dogs, ranging from dental chews and toys designed to scrape off plaque, to oral sprays and additives for their water. These products can supplement your brushing routine but shouldn't replace brushing entirely.

Professional dental cleanings are another key part of your dog's oral health regimen. Veterinarians perform dental prophylaxis, a thorough cleaning procedure performed under anesthesia. This procedure allows a comprehensive cleaning above and below the gumline and the ability to take X-rays, which is pivotal in identifying any underlying issues not visible to the naked eye.

Recognizing potential dental health issues early can save your dog from a lot of discomfort and prevent more serious health problems. Symptoms such as excessively bad breath, visibly inflamed or bleeding gums, a change in eating or chewing habits, abnormal drooling, pawing at the mouth, or a sudden decrease in appetite can all point to dental issues. A regular check of your dog's mouth at home for these signs and an annual veterinary dental check-up are crucial for early detection and treatment of dental problems.

Investing time and effort into your dog's dental hygiene will pay dividends in their overall health and wellbeing. A combination of at-home care and professional cleanings, coupled with a vigilant eye for any signs of dental issues, is the winning formula for maintaining your dog's oral and overall health. Keep in mind that preventative care is not just more cost-effective than treatment; it also saves your pet from unnecessary pain and discomfort. Always remember that a healthy mouth equates to a healthier, happier pup.

Vaccinations

The health and wellbeing of your dog hinge significantly on their vaccinations, making it a non-negotiable aspect of responsible pet ownership. This critical component of your puppy's healthcare regimen shields them from numerous potentially severe or fatal diseases. Here, we delve into the importance of vaccinations, discussing the essential vaccines your pup needs and their corresponding schedules.

Importance of Vaccinations
Immunization is paramount in the fight against several infectious diseases that could afflict dogs. Vaccines work by introducing a safe, controlled amount of a specific virus or bacteria to the dog's immune system. This exposure provokes the immune system to produce antibodies, providing it with a 'memory' of how to combat that particular pathogen. Consequently, if the vaccinated dog encounters the disease-causing pathogen later, their immune system promptly springs

into action, neutralizing the infection and preventing or lessening the disease's impact. The role of vaccinations extends beyond the individual dog. When a substantial portion of the dog population is vaccinated against contagious diseases, it creates a collective immunity that curbs the spread of these illnesses in the community. This protection is crucial for vulnerable dogs that cannot receive certain vaccinations due to age or health conditions.

Essential Vaccinations and Their Schedules

Vaccinations for dogs can be classified into two main categories: core and non-core vaccines. The former are universally recommended due to the severity of the diseases they protect against, while the latter are administered based on a dog's unique risk factors, such as their environment, lifestyle, and travel habits.

- **Core Vaccines:** Core vaccines comprise Distemper, Canine Parvovirus, Canine Hepatitis, and Rabies. These are non-negotiable, irrespective of the dog's lifestyle or geographical location. The first three are typically combined into a single shot referred to as the DHLPP vaccine.

- **Non-core Vaccines:** Non-core vaccines, such as Bordetella, Leptospirosis, Lyme disease, and Canine Influenza, among others, are tailored to a dog's specific circumstances. If your dog is at risk of exposure to these diseases due to their lifestyle or location, your vet may recommend these vaccines.

- **Vaccination Schedules:** Puppy vaccinations typically commence between 6-8 weeks of age, with booster shots administered every 2-4 weeks until about 16 weeks old. This series bolsters their immunity as the passive immunity they derived from their mother's milk gradually declines. The Rabies vaccine is usually administered at around 12-16 weeks of age, followed by a booster a year later. After the puppy year, most vaccines are administered every one to three years, depending on local laws, the individual dog's risk assessment, and the type of vaccine. Please remember that the information provided here is general in nature.

It's paramount that you consult your vet who will consider your dog's age, medical history, environment, and lifestyle to curate a vaccination schedule tailor-made for them. Regularly adhering to this schedule can play a pivotal role in securing your dog's long-term health and preventing avoidable suffering. Vaccinations are a simple, cost-effective solution to grave health problems that underline the essence of proactive and conscientious pet ownership.

Prevention and Correction of Behavioral Issues

Addressing behavioral issues in dogs is a vast and critical part of their health and wellbeing. It's essential to understand that behaviors perceived as problems often originate from the dog's innate instincts or their reaction to certain situations. The key lies in managing these behaviors positively and constructively, fostering a balanced and fulfilling relationship between you and your furry companion.

- **Leash Pulling:**
  When your dog incessantly pulls on their leash during walks, it can transform a pleasant activity into a strenuous exercise. This issue stems from the dog's excitement and desire to explore. One effective technical solution is to use a no-pull harness or a head halter, which helps redirect the dog's attention and discourages pulling. Additionally, you can practice loose leash walking by rewarding your dog for walking close to your side and gradually increasing the duration of walks.

- **Chewing:**
  Puppies chew to explore their environment and alleviate the discomfort of teething. Older dogs chew to keep their jaws strong and their teeth clean. Provide appropriate chew toys made of durable materials such as rubber or nylon. You can also use interactive puzzle toys that dispense treats or food to keep your dog mentally stimulated. It's important to supervise your dog during chewing sessions and redirect them from inappropriate objects by offering a suitable alternative.

Eating Poop:

Eating poop, also known as coprophagia, is a behavior that many dog owners find disturbing. To prevent this, keeping your yard clean and promptly removing feces is crucial. Engage your dog in regular physical activities to satisfy their mental and physical needs. Additionally, feeding your dog a well-balanced diet with proper nutrients can help reduce the likelihood of coprophagia. If the behavior persists, it's recommended to consult with a veterinarian to rule out any underlying medical condition.

Jumping Up:

Dogs often jump up on people to greet them or seek attention. One technical solution is to teach your dog an alternative behavior, such as sitting, when they greet people. Practice this behavior consistently and reward your dog for sitting politely. Additionally, you can use a leash to control your dog's jumping behavior and redirect their attention to a command or task. It's important to ensure that all members of your household and visitors follow the same procedure to reinforce the training.

Barking:

While barking is a normal canine behavior, excessive barking can become an issue. Understanding why your dog is barking excessively is the first step towards resolving the problem. Technical solutions include desensitization and counter-conditioning. For example, if your dog barks at specific triggers, gradually expose them to the trigger at a low intensity and reward calm behavior. You can also use positive reinforcement training to teach your dog a "quiet" command, rewarding them for being silent. Additionally, anti-barking devices like citronella collars or ultrasonic bark deterrents can be used as a temporary measure in certain situations, but they should be used with caution and under guidance.

Growling:

Growling is a form of communication that indicates discomfort, fear, or territoriality. It's important never to punish your dog for growling, as it's their way of warning before potentially resorting to biting. Instead, try to

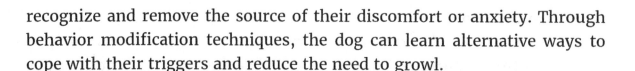

recognize and remove the source of their discomfort or anxiety. Through behavior modification techniques, the dog can learn alternative ways to cope with their triggers and reduce the need to growl.

Play Biting:

Puppies engage in play biting as a part of their learning and socialization. However, if your pup bites too hard during play, it's important to teach them bite inhibition. When your puppy bites too hard, let out a high-pitched yelp to startle them. This action mimics the response they would receive from another puppy during play, and it helps them understand that their bite was too hard. Immediately redirect their attention to a suitable chew toy or engage them in an alternative activity. Consistency in training and positive reinforcement for gentle play behavior are key to addressing this issue.

Begging:

To prevent begging, it's important to establish clear boundaries and consistency. Avoid giving your dog food from the table as it reinforces the begging behavior. Make sure your dog is well-fed with a nutritious diet before you sit down to eat. If necessary, train your dog to stay in another room or in their designated space during mealtimes. Reward your dog for calm and patient behavior during mealtime and provide them with interactive toys or puzzle feeders to keep them occupied.

Not Listening:

Training your dog to listen to commands requires consistency, patience, and positive reinforcement. Start with basic commands like 'sit,' 'stay,' and 'come' in a quiet and distraction-free environment. Use rewards such as treats, praise, or playtime when your dog responds correctly. Gradually increase the level of distractions and practice in different environments to generalize the commands. Consistency in training methods and clear communication will help your dog understand and respond to your cues effectively.

Submissive, Excited, and Marking Peeing:

These behaviors are often linked to the dog's emotional state or territorial instincts. For submissive or excited peeing, it's important to minimize overly exciting greetings or intimidating interactions. Approach your dog calmly and give them space to calm down before initiating any interactions. For marking, neutering or spaying your dog can help reduce the behavior, as can consistently house training and reinforcing appropriate elimination behaviors. Using belly bands or diapers can be helpful in managing marking behaviors indoors. Consistency, positive reinforcement, and patience are essential in addressing these issues.

Separation Anxiety:

Separation anxiety can lead to destructive behavior and distress for both the dog and the owner. Gradually acclimating your dog to being alone is crucial. Start with short periods of separation and gradually increase the duration as your dog becomes more comfortable. Create a positive association with your departures by providing special toys or treats that are only given when you leave. Use calming techniques such as leaving soothing music or a shirt with your scent to comfort your dog. In severe cases, consult with a professional dog trainer or a certified veterinary behaviorist for a comprehensive behavior modification plan.

Aggression:

Aggression in dogs can stem from fear, territoriality, resource guarding, or other underlying causes. It's crucial to address aggression with the help of a professional dog behaviorist or a veterinary behaviorist. They can assess the specific triggers and develop a behavior modification plan tailored to your dog's needs. Treatment may involve counter-conditioning, desensitization, positive reinforcement training, and management strategies to ensure the safety of both the dog and the people around them.

Common Fears: Loud Sounds, Being Left Alone, Certain People, Vacuum Cleaner, the Bathtub:

Desensitization and counter-conditioning techniques can be effective in managing common fears in dogs. Gradually expose your dog to the source of their fear in a controlled and positive manner. For example, if your dog is afraid of loud sounds, start by playing recordings of soft sounds at a low volume and gradually increase the volume over time. Pair the sounds with positive experiences, such as treats or playtime, to create a positive association. Similarly, if your dog is afraid of the vacuum cleaner, start by keeping it stationary and rewarding calm behavior. Gradually introduce movement while rewarding your dog for remaining calm. Consistency and patience are key in helping your dog overcome their fears.

Understanding and addressing your dog's behavioral issues not only leads to a well-behaved pet but also contributes to their overall health and wellbeing. It's important to remember that every dog is unique, and the solutions may vary based on their individual needs. Consulting with a professional dog trainer or a certified veterinary behaviorist can provide tailored guidance and support to ensure a happy and harmonious coexistence between you and your furry friend.

Upgrade your dog training journey with our **FREE BONUS** "*Well-Behaved Companion Program*". This unique program equips you with all the essential tools to train your dog effectively and overcome common canine challenges. Say goodbye to pet parenting hurdles and welcome a joyful bond with your four-legged friend. The secret to your dog's best behavior is just a scan away! Use **the QR code provided at the end of this book** to access and start enhancing your pet companionship experience today.

In the next part of the guide I cover how to maintain your dog's training and behavior over time. I provide tips on how to reinforce good behavior, prevent bad habits from forming, and troubleshoot common training problems. Additionally, I offer guidance on how to continue training your dog as they age and how to adjust their training as their needs change. Throughout this section, I emphasize the importance of consistency and patience in maintaining your dog's training and building a strong bond with them over time.

Smart Dog Training Secrets:
Unlocking Time and Money-Saving Techniques
for the Perfect Family Companion

Welcome to the world of Smart Dog Training Secrets! Are you ready to uncover the strategies that will help you save both time and money while transforming your beloved canine into the perfect family companion? In this comprehensive section, we will reveal a treasure trove of powerful techniques and valuable tips that will revolutionize your dog training journey. Say goodbye to costly trainers and hours of frustration—get ready to embark on an exciting training adventure that will enhance your dog's behavior and strengthen the bond between you and your furry friend. Let's dive in and discover the secrets of Smart Dog Training!

Assessing Your Training Goals

1. Define your desired training outcomes and prioritize the skills you want your dog to learn.
2. Set achievable milestones to track your progress and celebrate successes along the way.

Effective Training Techniques

3. Implement positive reinforcement techniques to motivate and reward your dog for desired behaviors.
4. Use clicker training to provide clear and consistent communication during training sessions.
5. Practice consistency and establish clear boundaries to promote a well-behaved and obedient dog.

Time-Saving Training Strategies

6. Optimize training sessions by focusing on short, frequent bursts of activity rather than lengthy sessions.
7. Incorporate training into everyday activities and routines to maximize your time and reinforce learning throughout the day.
8. Use targeted training exercises that address specific behaviors and problem areas efficiently.

Budget-Friendly Training Tips

9. Explore free or low-cost training resources, such as online tutorials, books, and community training classes.
10. Create DIY training tools and agility equipment using household items to save on expensive training gear.
11. Utilize everyday objects and environmental stimuli to create enrichment activities that stimulate your dog's mind.

Problem-Solving Techniques

12. Identify common training challenges and implement targeted solutions to address them effectively.
13. Seek advice from experienced trainers or behaviorists for personalized guidance on specific behavioral issues.
14. Stay patient, persistent, and positive throughout the training process, understanding that every dog learns at their own pace.

Congratulations! You now hold the key to Smart Dog Training Secrets that will not only save you time and money but also transform your family dog into the perfect companion. By utilizing the powerful techniques and valuable tips in this guide, you can unlock a world of training possibilities and create a harmonious bond with your furry friend. Get ready to embark on an exciting journey that will bring joy, fulfillment, and lifelong memories with your well-trained and happy canine companion.

PART V

DOG TRICKS

"To his dog, every man is Napoleon; hence the constant popularity of dogs."
—Aldous Huxley

As we delve into the captivating world of dog tricks, it's vital to understand the profound impact they can have beyond the obvious entertainment value. Dog tricks play an essential role in bonding, promoting mental and physical health, and facilitating effective communication between you and your furry friend. Teaching tricks to your dog extends far beyond a mere repertoire of amusing party stunts. It represents an opportunity for shared learning and engagement, which can significantly improve your dog's overall quality of life. It provides a form of mental stimulation that can help keep your dog's cognitive abilities sharp. Indeed, tricks challenge your dog to think, problem-solve, and engage with you on a level that goes beyond basic obedience commands.

Each time your dog learns a new trick, they are using their brain in ways they may not typically do during their everyday routine. This mental exercise helps to maintain cognitive function, promotes adaptability, and can even stave off cognitive decline in older dogs. Just like us, dogs can suffer from boredom, and teaching them tricks provides an enriching activity that keeps their minds active and engaged. In addition to the mental benefits, trick training can contribute to your dog's physical health. Many tricks, such as 'roll over', 'dance', or 'fetch', require dogs to use various muscle groups and engage in physical activity. This form of active play can aid in maintaining a healthy weight, building muscle tone, and improving overall fitness.

Apart from its health benefits, teaching tricks serves as an excellent bonding experience. Working together to learn a new trick can enhance trust and mutual understanding. It provides one-on-one time where both you and your dog can learn to understand each other better, ultimately strengthening your bond. Your shared accomplishments will instill a sense of pride and companionship in both of you.

Moreover, trick training establishes an effective communication pathway between you and your dog. As you guide them through a new trick, you both must understand each other's signals and cues, enhancing your communication skills. Your dog learns to pay close attention to your commands, and you become more attuned to your dog's body language and responses. In essence, teaching tricks to your dog is an enriching experience that promotes mutual respect and understanding. It fosters a stronger bond between you and your furry companion while contributing significantly to their mental and physical wellbeing. As we progress through this chapter, we'll explore numerous fun, challenging, and enjoyable tricks that will undoubtedly add laughter and joy to your shared time, while also reaping these incredible benefits.

Basic Tricks

Beg or Sit Pretty

In the 'Beg' or 'Sit Pretty' trick, your dog will sit up on their hind legs, creating a pose that many find endearing. However, this trick isn't just about cute photos for social media; it's a wonderful way to enhance your dog's balance and strengthen their core and hind legs. Before starting, ensure you have some bite-sized treats ready as a reward. Now, let's get into the training steps:

1. Ask your dog to 'Sit'. It's essential that your dog can comfortably sit before moving on to more advanced tricks.

2. Hold a treat above your dog's head, just out of their reach. The idea is to entice them to lift their front paws off the ground. Make sure you're not holding it too high that they might jump up to get it.

3. As soon as your dog lifts their front paws off the ground, even a little, reward them with the treat and praise them. This reinforces the action you want them to associate with the trick.

4. Add the command word 'Beg' or 'Sit Pretty' once your dog is comfortable with the trick. Make sure you say the command as your dog is doing the action.

5. Keep the training sessions short and sweet, to prevent your dog from getting bored or frustrated. Always end on a positive note.

6. Remember, some dogs may find this trick physically challenging, especially if they are overweight, older, or have joint issues. Always consult with your vet if you're unsure.

Reach Up

'Reach Up' is another delightful trick that promotes balance and strength. The goal here is to teach your dog to stretch their front legs upwards while keeping their hind legs firmly on the ground. Follow these steps to train your dog to 'Reach Up':

1. Start with your dog in a 'Sit' position.

2. Hold a treat above your dog's head, slightly further away than you would for 'Beg' or 'Sit Pretty', encouraging your dog to stretch upward.

3. As soon as your dog stretches up and their front paws are off the ground, reward them with the treat and praise.

4. Once your dog is reliably performing the action, add in the command word 'Reach Up'.

5. Again, keep sessions short and always end on a positive note.

Crawl

Crawling is an adorable trick where your dog moves forward while staying low on their belly. It's a delightful trick to show friends and family, and it also helps to increase your dog's body awareness. Follow these steps to train your dog to 'Crawl':

1. Start with your dog in the 'Down' position. If your dog isn't comfortable with this position, practice it before attempting to train the 'Crawl' command.

2. Hold a treat in your closed hand and place it near your dog's nose, but don't let them eat it. The goal is to lure your dog forward with the scent of the treat.

3. Slowly move your hand forward along the ground, encouraging your dog to crawl forward to follow the treat. If your dog stands up, go back to the 'Down' position and try again.

4. Once your dog starts to crawl forward, even a little, say the command 'Crawl', give them the treat and praise them enthusiastically.

5. Repeat these steps in short training sessions, gradually increasing the distance your dog has to crawl before they get the treat.

6. Over time, your dog will associate the word 'Crawl' with the action of moving forward while staying low on their belly.

7. Remember, patience and consistency are the keys to success in trick training.

Fetch

Fetch is a classic dog game that doubles as a trick. It involves your dog retrieving an object, such as a ball or a stick, and bringing it back to you. This activity is an excellent way to provide both physical exercise and mental stimulation for your dog. Here's how you can train your dog to 'Fetch':

1. Start with your dog's favorite toy and throw it a short distance away. Don't throw it too far; the idea is to get your dog interested in the object.

2. Encourage your dog to go after the toy with phrases like 'Get it!'. Celebrate verbally when they approach or touch the toy.

3. If your dog picks up the toy, celebrate their success with verbal praise, but don't try to take the toy away just yet.

4. Next, encourage your dog to come back to you with the toy. You can pat your legs, show them a treat, or use a happy voice to coax them back to you.

5. Once they return, ask them to 'Drop it' by holding a treat near their nose. Most dogs will drop the toy to take the treat. When they do, say 'Drop it' and give them the treat.

6. As your dog gets the hang of 'Fetch', you can gradually increase the distance that you throw the toy.

Paw Shake

An absolute classic in the realm of dog tricks, the 'Paw Shake' or 'Handshake' involves your dog lifting their paw to 'shake hands' with you or a willing volunteer. Not only is this trick adorable and crowd-pleasing, but it's also a nice way of teaching your dog politeness and cooperation. Here's how to train your dog to give a 'Paw Shake':

1. Begin with your dog in a 'Sit' position. Make sure this command is solid before attempting to add in the 'Paw Shake'.

2. Hold a treat in your hand and close your fist around it. Present your fist to your dog, near their chest level or slightly below.

3. Most dogs will naturally try to paw at your hand to get the treat. The moment your dog lifts their paw (even slightly), say 'Shake', open your hand to give them the treat, and lightly grasp their paw in a shaking motion.

4. Repeat this process regularly. Each time your dog successfully lifts their paw when you present your closed fist, reinforce the action with the 'Shake' command, followed by a treat and praise.

5. Once your dog consistently lifts their paw for the 'Shake' command, you can start to phase out the treat in your closed fist and just use your empty hand as a signal.

Remember, the aim is not to make your dog do tricks unwillingly, but rather to create a fun and stimulating activity that you can enjoy together.

Roll Over

'Roll Over' is a fantastic trick for enhancing your dog's agility and body awareness. It's also quite amusing to watch, which makes it a great trick for entertaining guests or children. Follow these steps to teach your dog to 'Roll Over':

1. Have your dog start in the 'Down' position. Make sure your dog is comfortable in this position before you start.

2. Hold a treat in your hand and show it to your dog. Then, move your hand slowly over your dog's shoulder to make your dog turn its head to follow the treat.

3. As your dog's body begins to follow its head, continue moving your hand in the direction you want your dog to roll. Say the command 'Roll Over' during this movement.

4. Once your dog completes a full roll, give them the treat and shower them with praise.

5. Repeat this regularly. With time, your dog will begin to associate the 'Roll Over' command with the action.

6. As your dog becomes more comfortable with the trick, you can start to phase out the treat and rely solely on the 'Roll Over' command.

Chores as Tricks

In this section, we're diving into two more handy tricks that will not only amuse and impress, but also provide practical benefits around your home. We will learn tricks that will help your dog actively participate in daily routines, boosting their sense of purpose and improving their skills in object retrieval.

Newspaper Delivery

Imagine the joy of starting your morning with your furry friend fetching the newspaper right at your doorstep. 'Newspaper Delivery' is a useful trick that combines the physical activity of fetching with a bit of domestic utility. To train your dog to deliver the newspaper, follow these steps:

1. Begin with a soft toy or rolled up paper that your dog is comfortable picking up, and gradually move to an actual newspaper once your dog gets the hang of the trick. Say the command 'Fetch' and throw the toy or paper.

2. When your dog picks up the item, use the command 'Come' to call them back to you. Offer treats and praise for successful retrieval.

3. Once your dog has mastered fetching and returning the item to you, introduce the actual newspaper. Let your dog see and smell the newspaper, making sure they're comfortable with it.

4. Practice the same 'Fetch' and 'Come' commands with the newspaper. Reward your dog for successful retrieval with treats and praise.

5. Finally, practice this routine by placing the newspaper outside the door. Open the door and command your dog to 'Fetch' the newspaper. Remember to reward them generously when they bring it back successfully.

Get Your Leash

The 'Get Your Leash' trick is another practical command that will come in handy daily. Your dog fetching their leash signals it's time for a walk, making your life a little easier and making walks a more collaborative event. Here's how to teach your dog this trick:

1. Start by showing your dog the leash and saying the command 'Get Your Leash'. Make sure they sniff the leash and get comfortable with it.

2. Once they touch the leash with their nose or mouth, reward them with a treat and praise. This will help them associate the action with the command.

3. Place the leash slightly farther away each time. Encourage your dog to fetch the leash with the command 'Get Your Leash'. Each time they successfully retrieve it, reward them.

4. Finally, place the leash in its usual spot and command 'Get Your Leash'. Encourage and reward your dog when they bring the leash to you.

Take and Drop it

One clever chore-based trick that helps keep your home tidy involves training your dog to pick up their toys. This trick not only teaches them to take responsibility but also provides mental stimulation. Let's see how it can be imparted:

- **Introduce the Basket:** Show your dog the basket where their toys should go. Let them sniff it and get used to it.

- **Master the 'Take' Command:** Use a toy your dog loves and present it to them saying the command 'take.' When they take it in their mouth, give them a treat and praise them.

- **Introduce the 'Drop It' Command:** Now, place the basket near your dog, say 'drop it' and guide the toy from your dog's mouth to the basket. You can gently touch their mouth to encourage them to let go of the toy. When they do, give them a treat and praise them.

- **Combine 'Take' and 'Drop It':** Now it's time to put it all together. Ask your dog to 'take' the toy and then walk them over to the basket and say 'drop it.' Each time they perform correctly, give them a treat and praise them.

- **Practice Regularly:** Keep practicing this sequence until your dog has mastered it. Over time, you can start to phase out treats, offering them only intermittently once your dog has the trick down.

Yard Clean

Another practical trick that can be a great help, particularly for those with large yards, is training your dog to help with yard work. For instance, you can train them to collect small branches or leaves in a specific area of your yard.

- **Introduce the 'Yard Clean' Command:** Choose a small object that your dog can easily pick up and give them the command to 'take.' When they take the object, say 'yard clean.'

- **Master the 'Drop It' Command:** Designate a specific area in your yard where you want your dog to drop the objects they pick up. Use the 'drop it' command and guide the object from your dog's mouth to the designated spot. Each time they perform correctly, give them a treat and praise them.

- 🐾 **Combine 'Yard Clean' and 'Drop It':** Now ask your dog to 'take' an object with the 'yard clean' command, lead them over to the designated spot and say 'drop it.' If they perform correctly, give them a treat and praise them.

- 🐾 **Practice with Various Objects:** Once your dog is comfortable with the sequence, introduce the objects you really want them to pick up, like small branches. Make sure these objects are safe for your dog to handle.

- 🐾 **Practice Regularly:** Consistent practice is crucial for your dog to master this trick. Always supervise this activity to ensure your dog's safety.

Funny Tricks

As we venture further into the delightful world of dog tricks, we will now explore a lighter, more playful facet. This section introduces some amusing tricks that extend beyond the realm of practical utility. The aim here is dual-faceted – enhancing your pup's skills and stimulating their mental capacities, all while bringing an element of entertainment into your daily interactions with your furry friend.

Doggy Push-ups

'Doggy Push-ups' is an entertaining trick that not only provides a good chuckle but also keeps your dog physically active and mentally engaged. This trick is a quick combination of 'sit', 'down', and 'stand' commands. Before starting, ensure your dog is familiar with these basic commands. Here's how to get your dog doing push-ups:

1. Begin with your dog in a standing position. Give the 'sit' command.

2. Once your dog sits, quickly follow it with the 'down' command, instructing your dog to lie down.

3. Next, give the 'stand' command to get your dog back on their feet.

4. Repeat these commands in quick succession. Encourage your dog to change their positions quickly, mimicking the action of a push-up.

5. Don't forget to reward your dog after a series of successful 'push-ups' with treats or praise.

6. Remember, it's important not to overdo this trick. Monitor your dog and ensure they're comfortable performing these actions repeatedly.

Play the Piano

This trick, while requiring a bit more effort, offers great amusement. Having your dog play the piano not only stuns onlookers but also serves as a testament to the amazing learning capabilities of dogs. Ensure that the keyboard or piano is safely placed at a level accessible to your dog. Follow these steps to teach your dog to 'Play the Piano':

1. Begin by drawing your dog's attention to the piano keys. You can do this by tapping the keys yourself or placing a treat on the keys to spark curiosity.

2. Encourage your dog to touch the keys. You can use a command such as 'Play' to cue the action. When your dog presses a key with their paw or nose, give them a treat and heaps of praise.

3. Repeat the process, each time encouraging your dog to press the keys with the 'Play' command. Always reward successful attempts.

4. Once your dog is comfortable pressing the keys on command, add a musical flair by teaching them to press different keys. You can guide their paws to different keys and reward them for following your direction.

5. With patience and practice, your dog will soon be impressing guests with their musical talents!

Spin and Twirl

This trick involves your dog spinning around in a circle, first one way (Spin), and then the other way (Twirl).

1. Start with a Treat in Your Hand: Hold a treat in your hand and let your dog sniff it. You want to get their attention focused on the treat.

2. Lead Your Dog in a Circle: Move your hand slowly in a circular motion close to your dog's nose, encouraging them to follow the treat and spin around in a circle.

3. Introduce the Command: Once your dog follows your hand and completes a full circle, say the command "Spin!" and then reward them with the treat and verbal praise.

4. Repeat and Practice: Keep repeating this, gradually removing the lure of the treat and relying on the command itself.

5. Introduce 'Twirl': Once your dog masters 'Spin,' you can teach 'Twirl' the same way but in the opposite direction.

6. Master the Trick: With regular practice, your dog will be able to Spin and Twirl on command, providing a fun and engaging spectacle!

Speak and Whisper

This trick consists of your dog barking on command (Speak), and then making a quieter sound, like a soft woof (Whisper).

1. Elicit a Bark: Wait for your dog to naturally bark, usually in response to a doorbell or knock. As soon as they do, say "Speak!", and reward them with a treat.

2. Repeat and Practice: Repeat this several times until your dog begins to understand that "Speak!" means to bark. Remember to give a treat each time they successfully bark on command.

3. Teach 'Whisper': Once 'Speak' is learned, hold a treat in your closed hand and let your dog sniff it but don't let them have it. They will likely whine or make softer noises out of frustration. At this moment, use the command 'Whisper' and reward them with the treat.

4. Master the Trick: Repeat this until your dog associates the softer noise with the 'Whisper' command.

5. As always, the goal is to have fun and enjoy the process. Remember, consistency and patience are key to successful training.

Dancing Tricks

Let's now delve into the energetic realm of dancing tricks that are bound to captivate audiences and enrich your dog's repertoire. It's important to note that these tricks often require a more complex set of movements and might take a bit longer for your dog to master. However, with patience, consistency, and loads of positive reinforcement, you'll be amazed at your dog's innate ability to perform these entertaining moves.

Our first dancing trick is the legendary Moonwalk. Made famous by Michael Jackson, this trick involves training your dog to slide their hind legs backward, mimicking the illusion of walking forward while moving in reverse. This trick is not only entertaining to watch but also a good way to help your dog improve their balance and coordination. Training your dog to Moonwalk involves the following steps:

1. Start by getting your dog to stand on their hind legs. You can do this by holding a treat above their head and slowly moving it backward. Reward your dog when they manage to balance on their hind legs.

2. Once your dog is comfortable standing on their hind legs, encourage them to move backward. You can achieve this by slowly moving the treat further back over their head. As your dog reaches for the treat, they will naturally move backward. Remember to reward them each time they make a backward movement.

3. The final step is to smooth out the movements. This will take time and practice. Keep practicing the trick in short sessions over several days or weeks. With enough repetition, your dog will start to perform the Moonwalk more fluidly.

Our second dance trick is the Chorus Line Kicks. This trick involves teaching your dog to kick one leg at a time in a walking motion. It's an excellent exercise for your dog's leg muscles and is sure to delight anyone who sees it. Here's how to train your dog to do the Chorus Line Kicks:

1. Start by training your dog to lift their paw on command. You can do this by touching their paw and rewarding them when they lift it. Practice this until your dog can consistently lift their paw on command.

2. Once your dog can lift their paw, the next step is to get them to move forward while doing so. You can encourage this by holding a treat in front of them and moving it forward as they lift their paw.

3. The final step is to get your dog to alternate their paws while moving forward. This can be done by alternating the paw you touch and reward.

4. Just like with the Moonwalk, this trick requires practice and patience. Keep your training sessions short and always end on a positive note.

Love Expressing Tricks

Here, we're focusing on those adorable gestures that not only reflect the bond between you and your furry friend but also melt hearts and draw smiles from all who witness them. A loving nudge, a tail wag, or a snuggle are ways in which your dog naturally expresses affection. However, there are a couple of other endearing tricks that you can teach your dog to reinforce this bond of love and make their affection visible to others.

Firstly, we have the 'Kisses' trick. It's quite a simple trick but one that always melts hearts. By teaching your dog to give kisses on command, you create a precious way for them to show their affection, whether it's to you, your family members, or even friendly strangers who would enjoy a little puppy love. Here's how you can train your dog to give kisses on command:

1. Get a small dab of peanut butter or a lickable treat and put it on your cheek. Say the command "kiss" and let your dog lick it off. This will get them associating the command with the action.

2. Repeat the previous step several times until your dog gets used to the command. Eventually, you can start giving the command without the treat. Remember to give lots of praise when your dog follows the command correctly.

3. With enough repetition, your dog will learn that "kiss" means to give a gentle lick, even when no treat is present. Remember to encourage your dog's progress with lots of positive reinforcement.

The second trick in this chapter is the 'Wave Goodbye.' This charming trick is a fun way to end interactions and leaves a lasting impression on anyone who experiences it. Here's how you can train your dog to wave goodbye:

1. Start by perfecting the 'Paw Shake' trick, as this forms the basis for 'Wave Goodbye'. Once your dog can confidently offer their paw for a handshake, you're ready to move on to the next step.

2. Hold out your hand as if you're going for a paw shake but keep it slightly out of your dog's reach. Your dog should lift their paw to try and reach your hand.

3. As your dog lifts their paw and realizes they can't reach your hand, they will likely start to move their paw in a waving motion. At this point, introduce the command 'Wave Goodbye' or simply 'Wave'.

4.   Give your dog a treat and lots of praise each time they successfully wave. Practice this trick consistently, and your dog will soon be waving goodbye on command.

As we draw to the close of our journey through the exciting world of dog tricks, it's time to take a step back and appreciate the overarching benefits of this rewarding process. Through the various chapters, we have seen how trick training contributes to the physical health, mental well-being, and overall happiness of our canine companions. But the benefits go beyond just the practical aspects; they have a profound impact on the bond between us and our four-legged family members. Teaching tricks to your dog isn't merely about creating entertaining party stunts, though these certainly bring a lot of joy and laughter. It's about spending quality time with your pet, offering them an outlet for their energy, and challenging their intellect. When you teach your dog a new trick, you're working as a team, fostering mutual trust and understanding. Moreover, the process of learning and performing tricks keeps your dog mentally sharp and physically agile. It's a form of mental and physical exercise that reduces anxiety and boredom, which can often lead to behavioral issues. When your dog is consistently engaged, they are happier, healthier, and less prone to developing destructive habits.

Beyond the health benefits, trick training is a way to communicate with your dog effectively. Each new trick your dog learns is a testament to the power of positive reinforcement and consistent, patient instruction. It's a silent conversation between you and your dog - one that deepens your bond and increases mutual respect. Finally, remember that every dog is unique, with their own set of strengths, weaknesses, and quirky personality traits. This individuality should shine through in their repertoire of tricks. Maybe your energetic Jack Russell Terrier has the perfect energy for fetching the newspaper, or perhaps your patient and gentle Labrador excels in giving affectionate kisses on command. These tricks can and should be tailored to suit your dog's individual capabilities and character traits.

CONCLUSION

As we conclude this enlightening journey into dog ownership and training, let's reflect on the lasting impressions and transformative takeaways. We've explored the multifaceted world of canine companionship, spanning from preparing our homes to the exhilarating process of teaching them tricks. Each step along this path has served to deepen the profound bond between us and our furry friends.

Remember, choosing to welcome a dog into your life is a commitment - to their health, their development, and their happiness. The training stages, which reach far beyond basic obedience and into the realm of expressive and engaging tricks, contribute significantly to a harmonious and fulfilling relationship with your pet. Furthermore, consistently meeting your dog's essential needs, ensuring regular physical activity and mental stimulation, and prioritizing their healthcare is foundational to their wellbeing.

In conclusion, owning a dog is a journey filled with mutual growth, challenges, joy, and, most importantly, unconditional love. As you move forward with the knowledge and insights you've gained from this book, we hope you will continue to explore, adapt, and grow alongside your canine companion. The journey with your furry friend is just beginning - treasure every moment of this adventure. After all, the love and companionship of a dog is one of life's greatest gifts.

Good luck, and cherish the journey,

Charlotte Marley

FAQ

Q1: At what age can I start training my dog?
A: You can begin basic training with puppies as young as 7-8 weeks old. It's essential to keep training sessions short, fun, and positive at this age. Focus on simple commands like sit, stay, and come.

Q2: How long should each training session last?
A: For young puppies, each session should last about 5 minutes to match their short attention spans. As the dog matures, training sessions can extend up to 15 minutes. Remember, consistency and regularity are key to reinforcing learning.

Q3: What if my dog doesn't seem to be interested in training?
A: Dogs may lose interest if they find the sessions too long or the exercises too complicated. Try breaking down the steps into smaller, achievable tasks. Incorporate more rewards, such as treats, toys, or praise, to keep your dog engaged. Make the training sessions interactive and fun.

Q4: Can old dogs be trained?
A: Absolutely! While older dogs may take a bit longer to learn new commands, they can certainly be trained. It's important to be patient and adjust the training methods to accommodate their age and physical abilities. Positive reinforcement and consistency are vital.

Q5: How can I stop my dog from barking excessively?
A: Excessive barking often stems from boredom, anxiety, or a need for attention. Identify and address the root cause of the barking. Provide mental and physical stimulation through interactive toys, regular exercise, and training activities. If the barking persists, seek professional help from a dog trainer or behaviorist.

Q6: How can I stop my dog from chewing on furniture or other items?
A: Chewing can be a sign of teething in puppies or boredom in adult dogs. Provide appropriate chew toys for your dog to redirect their chewing behavior. Supervise your dog closely and discourage chewing on furniture or inappropriate items by using safe, pet-friendly deterrent sprays or keeping those items out of reach.

Q7: My dog pulls on the leash during walks. How can I change this behavior?
A: Training your dog to understand and respond to leash pressure is essential. Use positive reinforcement to reward your dog when they walk nicely beside you without pulling. Incorporate techniques like stop-and-start or changing direction to teach your dog to walk on a loose leash. Consistency and patience are key to achieving leash manners.

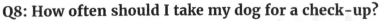

Q8: How often should I take my dog for a check-up?

A: Typically, adult dogs should have a vet check-up once a year. This allows the vet to assess their overall health, administer vaccinations, perform preventive care, and address any emerging issues. Puppies require more frequent visits for vaccinations and routine checks. Dogs with chronic health conditions or older dogs may benefit from more frequent check-ups as recommended by the vet.

Q9: How do I deal with my dog's aggressive behavior?

A: Aggression in dogs can stem from fear, dominance, possessiveness, or pain. It's important to identify the source of aggression and seek professional help from a certified dog trainer or a certified veterinary behaviorist. They can assess the specific triggers and develop a behavior modification plan tailored to your dog's needs. Punishment should never be used as it can escalate aggression.

Q10: How do I make my dog more sociable with other dogs and people?

A: Socialization should ideally start when your dog is a puppy. Expose them to various environments, people, and other animals in a controlled and positive way. Gradually increase the level of exposure as your dog becomes more comfortable. For adult dogs, socialization may take longer and require more patience. If your dog shows severe reactions or anxiety, consult with a professional trainer or a behaviorist who can guide you through a socialization program.

Q11: How can I prevent my dog from jumping on guests?

A: Jumping on guests is often a sign of excitement or a desire for attention. To discourage this behavior, teach your dog an alternative greeting behavior like sitting or staying. Reward your dog for calm and controlled behavior when guests arrive. Consistency and redirecting their energy towards a more appropriate behavior will help them understand the desired greeting behavior.

Q12: My dog is afraid of thunderstorms. What can I do to help them?

A: Thunderstorm phobia is common in dogs. Create a safe and comforting space for your dog during storms, such as a designated "safe zone" with their favorite toys and bedding. Play soothing music or use white noise to drown out the sound of thunder. Gradual desensitization and counter-conditioning techniques can also help your dog build a positive association with thunderstorms.

Q13: How do I stop my dog from digging up the yard?

A: Digging can be a natural behavior for dogs, but it can become a problem if they are ruining your yard. Provide your dog with a designated digging area filled with loose soil or sand. Encourage them to dig in that specific spot by burying toys or treats. Redirect their attention and energy to more appropriate activities like interactive play or mental stimulation.

Q14: How can I prevent my dog from resource guarding?
A: Resource guarding occurs when a dog displays possessive behavior over food, toys, or other items. Manage resource guarding by teaching your dog the "drop it" or "leave it" command and rewarding them for relinquishing objects. Avoid taking items away forcefully, as it can escalate the guarding behavior. Consult a professional dog trainer or behaviorist for a tailored behavior modification plan.

Q15: What can I do if my dog is experiencing separation anxiety?
A: Separation anxiety can cause distress in dogs when left alone. Gradually accustom your dog to being alone by practicing short absences and gradually increasing the duration. Provide them with interactive toys or treat puzzles to keep them mentally engaged while you're away. Consider using calming aids like pheromone diffusers or consulting a professional behaviorist for a comprehensive treatment plan.

UNLOCK EXTRA BONUSES!

Get ready for more than just a guide! **Scan these QR codes** that grant you immediate access to **additional exclusive bonuses**:

- **Workbook 1** FAST DOG AWAKENING & WBC Step-by-Step EXERCISE PROGRAM+INDOOR AND OUTDOOR PLAY GAMES

- **Workbook 2 Tips for Trips with Your Dog**

- **Workbook 3 Dog Training for Children**

- Workbook 4
  Homemade Ingenious Toys for Your Dog's Cognitive Health and Vitality

REFERENCES

American Kennel Club. (2021). *Dog Breeds.* https://www.akc.org/dog-breeds/

Animal Humane Society. (2021). *Dog Training.* https://www.animalhumanesociety.org/behavior/dog-behavior-and-training

Coren, S. (2005). *The Intelligence of Dogs: A Guide to the Thoughts, Emotions, and Inner Lives of Our Canine Companions.* Free Press.

Dibra, B., & Randolph, E. (1999). *Teach Your Dog to Behave: Simple Solutions to Over 300 Common Dog Behavior Problems from A to Z.* Penguin.

Dunbar, I. (2001). *Before and After Getting Your Puppy: The Positive Approach to Raising a Happy, Healthy, and Well-Behaved Dog.* New World Library.

Fogle, B. (2012). *Caring for Your Dog: The Complete Canine Home Reference.* DK ADULT.

Millan, C., & Peltier, M. J. (2008). *Cesar's Way: The Natural, Everyday Guide to Understanding and Correcting Common Dog Problems.* Three Rivers Press.

RSPCA Australia. (2021). *Dog Care.* https://www.rspca.org.au/take-action/dog-care

Scholten, A. (2002). *Home-Prepared Dog & Cat Diets: The Healthful Alternative.* Wiley-Blackwell.

IMAGES

1. <a href="https://www.freepik.com/free-photo/young-woman-training-french-bulldog-park_15589272.htm#query=dog%20training&position=11&from_view=search&track=ais">Image by serhii_bobyk</a> on Freepik

2. <a href="https://www.freepik.com/free-photo/bad-dog-making-mess_30999935.htm#query=dog%20home&position=4&from_view=search&track=ais">Image by pikisuperstar</a> on Freepik

3. Image by <a href="https://www.freepik.com/free-photo/supermarket-banner-with-various-items_29015664.htm#query=dog%20accessories&position=13&from_view=search&track=ais">Freepik</a>

4. Image by <a href="https://www.freepik.com/free-photo/young-couple-with-cute-dog_3357230.htm#query=dog%20training&position=14&from_view=search&track=ais">Freepik</a>

5. Image by <a href= "https://www.freepik.com/free-photo/close-up-veterinarian-taking-care-dog_18395502.htm#query=dog%20health&position=0&from_view=search&track=ais">Freepik</a>

6. Image by <a href= https://www.freepik.com/free-photo/beautiful-border-collie-dog-training-with-owner_23440131.htm#query=dog%20tricks&position=1&from_view=search&track=ais">Freepik</a>

Made in United States
North Haven, CT
28 September 2023

42100372R00070